UNIT	TOPIC	GRAMMAR	FUNCTION	VOCABULARY	READING	LISTENING	WRITING	SPEAKING	PRONUNCIATION
Introduction — Pages 6–7	English in Class / English you know	Imperatives	Classroom language	International words					
1 — Pages 8–13	New friends / Countdown: *numbers* / The OK Club	Imperatives / The verb *be* (singular) / *my, your*	Introductions	Countries / Numbers 0–10 / Phrases for warning and apologizing	Reading messages	Identifying countries, phone numbers	Writing about yourself / Writing messages	Introducing yourself	Saying phone numbers / Sentence stress in greetings / /iː/
2 — Pages 14–19	Looking around: *countries, classroom objects* / The Top Twenty / The OK Club	The verb be (plural) / *Who? What?* / Indefinite article: *a/an* / Demonstratives: *this/that*	Asking about people and objects / Asking about meanings of words	Classroom furniture and objects / Numbers 11–20	Checking statements	Identifying objects		Asking about age	Sentence stress in questions / /e/ and /iː/
3 — Pages 20–25	The living world / Families / The OK Club	*have got* / Plural nouns / Adjectives	Describing people and animals	Colours / Animals / Family members / Parts of the body	Checking statements / Matching texts and pictures / Finding information	Completing information / Identifying family members	Writing descriptions of animals / Writing a personal description	Describing your family / Discussing a problem	Intonation in questions and answers / /ə/ in *have* / /eɪ/ and /aɪ/
4 — Pages 26–31	At home / Shirts and skirts: *clothes* / The OK Club	*there is, there are* / Prepositions of place / Possessive *'s* / Possessive adjectives	Describing a house/rooms / Expressing opinions	Rooms / Furniture / Clothes	Checking information and details	Understanding a description / Identifying key information	Writing a description of your home	Giving opinions / Describing rooms	Word stress in questions and answers / /uː/, /ʌ/, /ɑː/ and /əʊ/
5 — Pages 32–37	The best of British: *food* / What would you like?: *menus* / The OK Club	The present simple / Countable and uncountable nouns / *some and any*	Expressing likes/dislikes and preferences / Talking about and ordering food	Food and drink / Ingredients / Prices / Numbers 21–100 / Nationalities	Skimming a text to identify topic and content / Reading and using a menu	Checking specific and general information	Describing a drink	Asking about cooking and eating / Ordering food in a cafe	Word and sentence stress in simple dialogues / /s/, /z/, /ɪz/
Consolidation 1 — Pages 38–41	Revision	Revision of grammar points	Revision of functions	Revision of vocabulary	Identifying topics in a letter	Identifying likes and dislikes	Completing notes / Completing a form / Writing a letter to a friend	Meeting p… / Offering and accepting food and drink	

UNIT	TOPIC	GRAMMAR	FUNCTION	VOCABULARY	READING	LISTENING	WRITING	SPEAKING	PRONUNCIATION
6 Pages 42–47	Life and times: *the lives of pop stars*; Carnival time: London's carnival; The OK Club	Adverbs of frequency; Present simple questions; Object pronouns	Describing routines; Telling the time	Music and dance	Skimming a text to identify topic and content	Identifying context; Finding specific information	Writing about routines; Writing an advert	Interviewing a pop singer; Describing someone's routine; Buying and selling	Word stress /æ/ and /ʌ/
7 Pages 48–53	Imagine this...: *space travel*; Clever inventions; The OK Club	Demonstratives: *this, that, these* and *those*; Quantifiers: *a little, a few,* and *a lot of*	Describing objects; Expressing quantity	Space travel; Shapes; Useful things at home or work	Matching text and pictures	Identifying key information; Matching descriptions with pictures	Writing puzzles; Writing a description of an invention	Discussing the purpose of objects; Describing the location of objects	/θ/ and /ð/; Word and sentence stress
8 Pages 54–59	That's amazing: *interesting facts*; Do you want to be a champion?; The OK Club	*can/can't must*; Prepositions of time	Expressing ability; Agreeing and disagreeing; Expressing obligation	Names of languages; Sports and hobbies; Days of the week	Matching text with pictures; Finding and checking information; Matching titles with paragraphs	Identifying context; Checking specific information; Correcting and completing information	Writing a short article	Checking facts; Asking about ability; Making arrangements	Word and sentence stress *can* and *can't*
9 Pages 60–65	Travelling: *coral reefs*; Having a wonderful time ...?; *holidays*; The OK Club	The present continuous; Adverbs of manner	Describing what is happening; Talking about the weather	The weather; Directions; Holidays	Finding information; Guessing meaning from context; Understanding mood	Identifying key information; Identifying main message; Identifying a speaker from manner and main message	Writing a postcard; Creating an extended dialogue	Discussing holidays; Checking information; Asking about spending habits; Buying a present	/ŋ/
10 Pages 66–71	Diet and lifestyle; Pocket money; The OK Club	The present simple and present continuous; *How much/many?* Ordinal numbers	Discussing lifestyles and spending choices	Everyday actions; Food; Numbers over 100; Per cent and fractions; Months and dates	Responding to a questionnaire; Finding and checking information	Completing a questionnaire; Understanding meaning from context; Checking specific information; Discriminating between numbers; Identifying context	Describing spending habits	Revising shop dialogues	Word and sentence stress; Ordinal numbers
Consolidation 2 Pages 72–75	Revision	Revision of grammar points	Revision of functions	Revision of vocabulary	Finding information to complete graphs	Checking information; Identifying key information	Writing a survey report	Discussing sports activities	

CPA

PACESETTER
STARTER

STUDENT'S BOOK

DEREK STRANGE   DIANE HALL

OXFORD
UNIVERSITY PRESS

Oxford University Press,
Great Clarendon Street,
Oxford OX2 6DP

Oxford   New York
Athens   Auckland   Bangkok   Bogotá
Buenos Aires   Calcutta   Cape Town   Chennai
Dar es Salaam   Delhi   Florence   Hong Kong
Istanbul   Karachi   Kuala Lumpur   Madrid
Melbourne   Mexico City   Mumbai   Nairobi
Paris   São Paulo   Singapore   Taipei   Tokyo
Toronto   Warsaw

and associated companies in
Berlin   Ibadan

OXFORD and OXFORD ENGLISH
are trade marks of Oxford University Press

ISBN 0 19 436325 2
ISBN 0 19 436843 2 (Turkish edition)

© Oxford University Press 2000

The publishers would like to thank the students of Mukogana Fort
Wright Institute, Spokane, WA, USA for the Japanese calligraphy
on p. 59.

Printed in China

Acknowledgements

Illustrations by: Mike Adams pp. 9, 10, 43, 47; Tony Ansell pp. 6,
10, 15, 17, 45, 73, 82, 83; Kathy Baxendale (handwriting) pp. 27,
35, 62, 68, 69, 83, 99; Brett Breckon pp. 16, 28, 29, 31, 53, 67, 81;
Chris Brown pp. 19, 60, 102; Nick Burke pp. 17, 19; Mark Draisey
pp. 48, 77, 85, 100, 101, 105; Nicki Elson pp. 8, 47, 87; Neil Gower
pp. 27, 31, 63, 65, 67, 84, 95, 108, 109; Kev Hopgood pp. 48, 49;
Tim Kahane pp. 15, 25, 65, 59, 74; Claire Littlejohn p. 96; Mac
McIntosh pp. 24, 36, 88, 93; Ian Moore pp. 20, 68, 85; Andrew
Peters pp. 7, 28, 37, 39, 51, 73, 103; Andrew Selby pp. 34, 35;
Raymond Turvey p. 50; Harry Venning pp. 25, 66, 71; Kath
Walker pp. 38, 53, 72, 106; Darrel Warner pp. 32, 33, 66.

Cover illustration: Sue Climpson.

Commissioned photography by: David Tolley pp. 22 (family
portrait) and 54 (dictionaries). All other photos by Bill Osment.
With additional thanks to: B & Q, Oxford; Cycle King,
Oxford; Faulkner's Garage; George and Davis Cafe; The Phoenix
Cinema, Oxford; The Jericho Cafe, Oxford; Oxford Film and
Video; Union Street, The Centre for Young People, East Oxford

Picture research by: Jane Taylor.

**The publishers would like to thank the following for their kind
permission to reproduce photographs**

Adams Picture Library p. 23 (Ela Mierzecka-Badran/black haired
man, Barry Clothier/fair haired man, Graham Horner/red haired
man); Associated Press p. 90 (Pierre Gleizes/Jacques Cousteau);
BBC p. 11 (logo); Biofotos p. 21 (Heather Angel/stick insect, arctic
fox, tarantula); Anthony Blake Photo Library p. 30 (Gerrit Bunt);
Camera Press p. 44 (Lennox Smillie); J.Allan Cash Photo Library
p. 23 (man with moustache); Eye Ubiquitous p. 40 (Pam
Thompson/house); Ronald Grant Archive pp. 14 (Holmes &
Watson,MGM/Three Musketeers), 89 (Warners/Stephen
Spielberg); Robert Harding Picture Library pp. 62 (beach &
mountains), 96 (W. Rawlings/Tower of London); The Kobal
Collection p. 12 (*Catwoman*); London Features International
p. 33 (Colin Mason); London Zoo p. 96 (logo); Macmillan
General Books p. 89 (book cover); Paul Mulcahy pp. 15 (back pack
& pencil), 42, 90 (aqualung), 100; NASA/Genesis Space Photo
Library p. 10; NHPA pp. 21 (Kevin Schafer/giraffe, Daniel
Heuclin/glass lizard), 40 (Patrick Fogot/cats), 54 (Stephen
Dalton/lizard, Karl Switak/piranha); News International
Associated Services Ltd p. 94 (Dan Callis/*The Times*); "PA" News
Photo Library p. 78; Rex Features pp. 14 (Pierce Brosnan as
James Bond, Mel Gibson as *Braveheart, The Simpsons*), 15 (Pierce
Brosnan as *James Bond, Lisa Simpson*), 54 (woman blowing
bubble gum, scuba diving dog), 88, 91; Science Photo Library p. 9
(Tom Van Sant/Geosphere Project, Santa Monica); Tony Stone
Images pp. 23 (Penny Tweedie/girl, David Young-Wolf/man in
stripey top), 56, 61, 62 (Charlotte Saule/Tyrol), 94 (Buckingham
Palace); Mike Siegel p. 26; Stockmarket p. 76; Telegraph Colour
Library p. 54 (Planet Earth/Doug Terrine/sailfish); Tussaud Group
p. 96 (Mme Tussaud & Rock Circus logos); Vardon Attractions
p. 96 (London Dungeon logo).

English in class

1 🔊 Look at the pictures. Listen.

1

Good morning.

2

Listen.

3

Look at the example.

4

Don't look at the picture.

5

Say it again, please.

6

Thank you.

7

What does this mean?

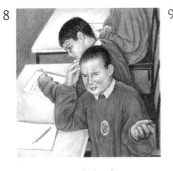

8

Excuse me. I don't understand.

9

Yes, that's right.

10

No, that's wrong.

11

Goodbye!

2 How do you say these things in your language?

3 a 🔊 Listen and write the number of the picture.

Example

A – 8

b Listen again and repeat.

4 Match the instructions with the pictures.

1 Write …   a 🔊

2 Read …   b 💬

3 Listen …   c ✏️

4 Work with a partner.   d 📖

English you know

1 a   Match the pictures with the English words.

cafe	✓
coffee	☐
cola	☐
computer	☐
doctor	☐
football	☐
hamburger	☐
pizza	☐
policeman	☐
restaurant	☐
sandwich	☐
taxi	☐
telephone	☐
television	☐
tennis	☐
train	☐
video	☐
yacht	☐

b   📼 Listen and repeat the words.

Learn to learn: using a vocabulary book

2 Organize new words in a vocabulary book.

Food and drink

hamburger   coffee

sandwich

Picture dictionary

Food and drink	
English	My language
coffee	------------
cola	------------
hamburger	------------
pizza	------------
sandwich	------------

List and translation

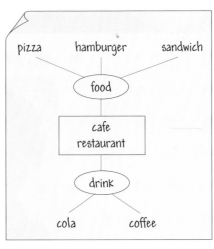

pizza   hamburger   sandwich

food

cafe
restaurant

drink

cola   coffee

Word-map

3 Add these words to your vocabulary book. Use the ideas in Exercise 2.

Australia bank basketball
Britain Canada cassette
cinema hotel Japan
lemonade museum park
secretary university volleyball

New friends

Introductions

1 a 📼 Listen.

Hello. My name's Kerry – Kerry Walker. What's your name?

Hi. I'm from Britain. Where are you from?

My name's Carol. Carol Hill. This is Dave.

I'm from Australia.

b Listen again and repeat.

2 📼 Listen and answer.

My name's … . I'm from … .

3 💬 Work with a partner.

A Hello. My name's … What's your name?
B Hi, … . My name's … .
A Where are you from?
B I'm from … . And you?
A I'm from … .

4 ✏️ Write about yourself.

What's your name?

My _____

_____

Where are you from?

I'm _____

_____

Where are you from?

1 Match the people with the countries.

1	Steve _____
2	Shannon _____
3	Levent _____
4	Magda _____
5	Eleni _____
6	Tina _____
7	Carlos _____

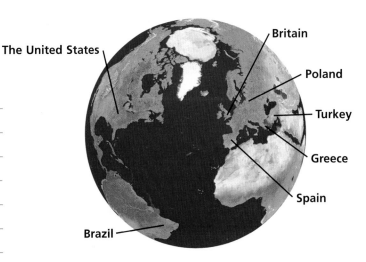

The United States · Britain · Poland · Turkey · Greece · Spain · Brazil

INTERNATIONAL STUDENTS' GROUP

Shannon · Levent · Magda · Eleni · Tina · Steve · Carlos

2 📼 Listen. Tick (✓) the countries you hear.

Argentina ☐ Brazil ☐ Britain ☐ Canada ☐
Greece ☐ Hungary ☐ Japan ☐ Mexico ☐
Poland ☐ Spain ☐ Turkey ☐ the United States ☐

3 💬 Choose one of the people. Ask and answer.

A Are you from Poland?
B No.
A Are you from Brazil?
B Yes.
A You're Tina!
B Yes, that's right.

4 a ✏️ Write introductions.

Example
This is Steve. He's from …

b Write introductions for two other students.

c Read your introductions to the class.

Work it out: the verb *be* (singular)

5 ✏️ Complete the chart.

Short forms	Long forms
I'___	I am
You ___	You are
He ___	He is
She ___	She is

6 a 📼 Listen. Where are they from?

b Listen again and repeat.

Countdown!

Numbers 0–10

1 a 🔊 Listen and repeat the numbers.

b Say the numbers from 1 to 10.

One … two …

c 🔊 Listen and say the numbers from 10 to 1.

Ten … nine … eight …

10 – 9 – 8 – 7 –
6 – 5 – 4 – 3 –
2 – 1 …

BINGO!

2 a 🔊 Write five numbers. Listen and tick (✓) the numbers you hear.

Example
Game 1

	1		3	
6		7		10

b Look at the picture. Play the game in groups. Take turns to say the numbers.

… four … two … nine … seven …

Bingo!

3 🔊 Listen and write the phone number.

Hello, Steve. This is Kerry, from Australia. I'm in London with my family – please phone me at my hotel. The number is _____ … bye!

Useful English 🔊

Phone numbers

648…2350 = six, four, eight … two, three, five, oh.

391 1927 = three, nine, one … one, nine, two, seven.

Hello. This is 917 8532.

Goodbye!

4 🔊 Listen and repeat the phone numbers.

Steve	648	2350
Shannon	917	8532
Levent	460	5917
Magda	837	4162
Tina	971	0253
Carlos	864	1627
Eleni	459	3298

5 🗩 Work with a partner.

a Listen and answer.

A My number's eight, three, seven … four, one, six, two.

B You're Magda.

A Yes, that's right.

b Write three numbers of your family or friends.

A Say one number. *Seven, two, three … eight, six, four, oh.*

B Write the number. *723 8640*

Take turns.

6 ✏️ Write these phone numbers in words.

Example
971 0253   Nine, seven, one … oh, two, five, three.

1   648 2359   2   989 2631   3   804 3066

How are you?

Useful English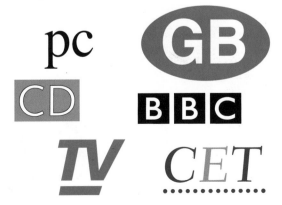

How are you?
I'm fine, thanks.
I'm very well, thanks.

1 Listen. Who are the two people on the phone?

| Carlos | Eleni | Levent | Magda | Shannon | Steve | Tina |

A Hello _____ .

B Hi, _____ . _____ is _____ here.

A Oh, hi, _____! Thanks for _____ message.
How are you?

B _____ fine, thanks. How are _____?

A _____ very well.

2 Listen again. Complete the dialogue.

3 Work with a partner. Make a new dialogue.

4 Read the fax message. Complete the sentences.

1   The message is from _____ .

2   His fax number is _____ .

3   The message is to _____ .

4   Her number is _____ .

FAX MESSAGE   Page 1 of 1
....
To: Tina Canto 638 0759
From: Steve Benson
Date: 3.3.2001
....
Dear Tina,
Thank you for your fax message. How are you? This is my
address:
7 Park Road
Oxford OX2 3DP
England
My phone and fax numbers are:
Telephone: [01865] 735 6924
Fax: [01865] 735 0188

---

5 Write a fax to Steve in Oxford.

FAX MESSAGE   Page 1 of 1
....
To: _____

[Fax number: _____]

From: _____

Date: _____
....
Dear _____ .

Thanks for _____

How are you?

This is my address: _____

_____

_____

Please write to me.

Pronunciation: /iː/ and /ɪ/

6 a   Look at these words: *he, she, please.*
Listen and repeat.

b   Listen and tick (✓) the words with the /iː/ sound:
with ☐ read ☐ listen ☐ is ☐ three ☐ me ☐

c   Listen and repeat the words with the /ɪ/ sound.

d   Listen and repeat these letters.
B, C, D, E, G, P, T, V

e   Say these letters.

pc   GB   CD   BBC   TV   CET

Pleased to meet you

1   **a**   Look at the story. Write introductions for the five people.

1   *This is ...*   2 _____   3 _____   4 _____   5 _____

b   Listen and read. Check your answers.

Speech bubbles in picture 4:

I'm Emma, Emma Starr. This is Jack Morris … and this is Ricky Sinclair!

Pleased to meet you. We're new here. I'm Carol Hill. And this is my brother, Dave.

Hi.

Speech bubble in picture 5:

Here's my number. Phone me later.

Set the pace

2 a Look at the pictures again. What do these things mean in your language? Make a guess.

1	Be careful!	3	I'm sorry.
2	Look out!	4	Pleased to meet you.

b Listen and repeat.

3 Work in groups. Practise the dialogue for picture 4. Take turns.

A You are Emma.   C You are Jack.
B You are Carol.   D You are Ricky.

Review

Commands

Positive	Negative
Say …	Don't say …

The verb *be* (singular)

Long forms	Short forms
I am	I'm
You are	You're
He is	He's
She is	She's
This is	—

1 Work with a partner. Complete the dialogue.

A Hello. I'___ Magda. What'___ your name?

B Hi, _____. My name'___ Mary Lou. I'____ _____ the United States. Where _____ _____ from?

A _____ from Poland. Oh, this _____ Carlos. _____ from Spain.

2 a Write a short dialogue with these sentences.

I'm fine, thanks.   Hi, …!   How are you?
How are you?   I'm fine, thank you.   Hello, ….

b Practise the dialogue with a partner.

Vocabulary

Look at the unit again. Add all the new words for countries and numbers to your vocabulary book.

Freewheeling ....

Find the names of ten other countries (→ or ↓).

M	**E**	**X**	**I**	**C**	**O**	B	H	F	A
E	N	G	L	A	N	D	U	J	U
G	T	K	S	N	H	R	N	P	S
R	U	S	P	A	I	N	G	O	T
E	R	N	F	D	V	B	A	L	R
E	K	C	G	A	W	K	R	A	A
C	E	H	M	Q	P	C	Y	N	L
E	Y	B	R	A	Z	I	L	D	I
K	A	R	G	E	N	T	I	N	A

Looking around

Where are they from?

1 Who is he/she? Who are they?

Examples
He's James Bond.
They're the Simpsons.

1 Who is he?

2 Who is she?

3 Who is he?

4 Who are they?

5 Who are they?

6 Who are they?

2 Where are they from?

America	Britain	France

Examples
He's from Britain.   They're from America.
I don't know.

3 a 📼 Listen and check the right answers.

   b 📼 Listen and repeat.

4 ✏️ Write about the people.

Example
Number one is James Bond. He's from Britain.

5 Who are you? Look at the pictures. Play the game in a group.

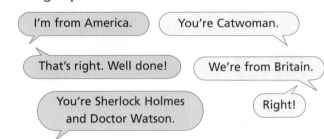

I'm from America.   You're Catwoman.

That's right. Well done!   We're from Britain.

You're Sherlock Holmes and Doctor Watson.   Right!

Work it out: the verb *be* (plural)

6 a ✏️ Complete the sentences.

   1 Bart and Lisa Simpson are from America.

     They _____ from America.

   2 I'm Carol and this is Dave. We _____ from England.

   b Complete the chart with the verb *be*.

We _____	
You _____	from Argentina.
They _____	

   c Correct the sentences.

Example
~~She~~ from Japan. *She's from Japan.*

1	We's from the United States.	3	They's from Poland.
2	She from Hungary.	4	Who're this?
		5	What that?

   d Put the apostrophe (') in the right places.

1	Shes from America.	4	Whos she?
2	Im from England.	5	Theyre from France.
3	Whats that?		

Your classroom

Learn to learn: using a dictionary (1)

1 Work with a partner. Choose one box, A or B, each. Use a dictionary and write the English words for the things in your box.

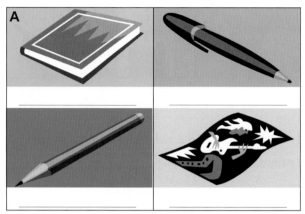

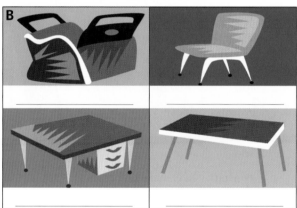

2 a Listen. Point to the things in your box only.

b Listen again. Repeat the things in your box.

Useful English

What's this in English?	Sorry, I don't know.
What does this mean?	

3 a Work with a partner. Ask about the things in your partner's box.

A What's this in English?
B It's a pencil. What's this in English?
A It's a ...

b Write the words in the other box.

c Complete the list on page 73 of the Workbook.

4 Ask about things in your classroom.

What's this in English?

I don't know.

Work it out: *Who ...?* or *What ...?*

5 a Complete the questions with *Who's* (Who is) or *What's* (What is).

1 _____ this? 2 _____ this?

3 _____ this? 4 _____ this?

b Complete the rule.

_____ is for people. _____ is for things.

6 Work with a partner. Ask and answer about people or things.

A What's this? A Right. ... Who's this?
B It's a chair. B She's Lisa Simpson.

The Top Twenty

Numbers 1–20

1 a 🔊 Listen. Repeat the numbers of the Top Twenty.

1	one	6	six	11	eleven	16	sixteen
2	two	7	seven	12	twelve	17	seventeen
3	three	8	eight	13	thirteen	18	eighteen
4	four	9	nine	14	fourteen	19	nineteen
5	five	10	ten	15	fifteen	20	twenty

b 🔊 Listen and write the missing numbers.

2 a 🗣 Work with a partner.

    A What's number thirteen?
    B Number thirteen is ... *Two Brothers*.

b Ask other questions.

    A What number is ... *My Friends*?
    B Mmm ... It's number eighteen.
    A Good! Well done!

How old are you?

1 Complete the dialogue.

    A How old are you?
    B I'm _____ . How old are you?
    A I'm _____ , too.

2 🗣 Ask five other students: *How old are you?* Write the answers.

Examples
Levent is fourteen and I'm fourteen, too – we're fourteen.
Magda is fifteen and Gemma is fifteen – they're fifteen.

3 ✏ You are in a video shop with a friend. Look at the videos. Complete the dialogues.

1   **You**   *Insect Man*, please.
      Woman   _____ _____ are you?
      You   _____ 're fifteen.
      Woman   No, sorry. _____ not eighteen.

2   **You**   *Two Brothers*, please.
      Woman   How _____ _____ you?
      You   We' _____ _____ .
      Woman   OK, here you are!

a / an

1 Look at the videos and read the sentences.

1   Number five is about **an** insect.
2   Number sixteen is about **an** animal.
3   Number seventeen is about **a** fish.
4   Number nineteen is about **a** bird.

2 Look at the videos again. What are they about?

an agent   an English woman   a city   a country

1   Number 6 is about _____ .
2   Number 4 is about _____ .
3   Number 2 is about _____ .
4   Number 20 is about _____ .

3 🗣 Work with a partner. Ask and answer questions.

    A What's number 1/2/3/ ... about?
    B It's about a .../an ...

Work it out: *a* and *an*

4 a Look at Exercises 1–3 again. When do we use *a*? When do we use *an*?

b Write the words in the correct list.

> animal ant bag book boy elephant girl operation pen student table

a	an
a game	an insect

c Check new words in a dictionary. Start a list of animals in your vocabulary book.

this and *that*

1 📼 Listen and look at the pictures from *Gulliver's Travels*. Answer the questions.

Example
Yes, it is or *No, it isn't.*

1 Is this an insect?

2 Is this an insect?

3 Is that an animal?

4 Is that an elephant?

Work it out: questions and short answers with *be*

2 a Look at the questions.

That's a bird.   He's from Poland.
Is that a bird?   Is he from Poland?

b Complete the questions.

Example
(I) *Am I* in this group?

1 (We) _____ _____ right?
2 (You) _____ _____ a student?
3 (They) _____ _____ seventeen?
4 (He) _____ _____ from France?
5 (She) _____ _____ fifteen?

c Write the rule for making questions with *be*.

3 Complete the short answers.
Is he/she from Japan? ✔ *Yes, he is.* ✘ *No, she isn't.*

1 Is she from the United States? _____.
2 Are they from Argentina? _____.
3 Is he from Mexico? _____.
4 Are they from Australia? _____.

4 🗨 Work with a partner. Look at the pictures in Exercise 1 for 20 seconds.

A (Don't close your book.) Is number four an insect?
B (Close your book.) Yes, it is./No, it isn't.

Pronunciation: /e/ and /i:/

5 a 📼 Listen and repeat these words.
yes desk ten

b 📼 Listen and tick (✓) the words with the /e/ sound.

desk ☐ coffee ☐ pen ☐ twelve ☐
he ☐ three ☐ friend ☐ me ☐

c 📼 Listen and repeat the other words.

d 📼 Listen and repeat these letters.

F, L, M, N, S, X, Z

Help! Fire!

1 What is a kettle? Use your dictionary. Find a kettle in the pictures.

2 📖 Listen, read and match.
Who are they? Dave Carol Jane

1 the girl at the Coffee Corner in the OK Club
2 the new boy
3 his sister

① Three days later

> Come to the club this evening. You and Dave – OK?

> **Carol** Yes, great! See you later. Bye!

②

Dave What is the OK Club?
Emma It's the club for young people here. We're all members of the OK Club – Ricky, Jack, me, Jane and …
Jack Yes – Jane. It's my turn at the Coffee Corner with Jane this evening.
Ricky Here we are. Welcome to the OK Club!

③

④

Jane Pleased to meet you, too, Dave. Coffee?
Dave Er … coffee? Oh, yes, please.

> Look at that smile! And it's for Dave! Oh no!

Jack Carol, this is Jane. Jane, this is Carol … and that's her brother, Dave. They're new here.
Jane Pleased to meet you, Carol.

⑤

Carol Help!
Jane Look! The kettle! It's on fire!
Dave It's OK! Don't worry!

3 a Look at the pictures again. How do you say these phrases in your language? Make a guess.

1 See you later!   3 Help!
2 Welcome!   4 Don't worry!

b 🔊 Listen and repeat.

4 Find responses to these phrases in the story.

1 Come to the club
   this evening.   _____

2 This is Carol.   _____

3 Coffee?   _____

4 It's on fire!   _____

Review

Subject pronouns; the verb *be*

Positive	Negative	Questions
I'm (I am)	I'm not	Am I …?
You're (You are)	You aren't	Are you …?
She's (She is)	She isn't	Is she …?
He's (He is)	He isn't	Is he …?
We're (We are)	We aren't	Are we …?
They're (They are)	They aren't	Are they …?

Wh- questions	
Who's … ? (Who is … ?)	Who are … ?
What's … ? (What is … ?)	What are … ?

a or *an*?

a	a video	a game
an	an animal	an insect

this or *that*?

This is Jane.   That's Jack.

1 Complete the sentences.

1 'Am _____ right?' 'No, _____ 're wrong – sorry!'

2 'Where's your sister?' '_____ isn't here.'

3 'Look at that fish – is _____ a shark?'

4 'Carol, _____ 're in group one.'

5 'Jack and Dave … _____ 're in group two.'

2 Write *a* or *an*.

1 _____ example   3 _____ English book

2 _____ student   4 _____ game

3 Write *What's this?* or *What's that?*

1 _____   2 _____

Vocabulary

Look at the unit again. Write all the new words for things in the classroom, numbers 11-20 and animal names in your vocabulary book.

Freewheeling ....

Write these numbers in the boxes.

zero	one	four	five	eight	nine

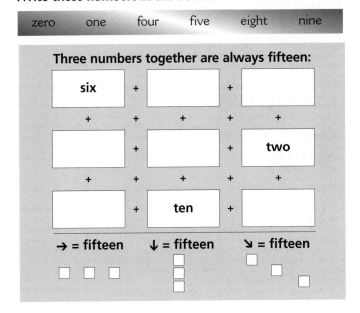

Three numbers together are always fifteen:

six	+		+	
+	+	+	+	+
	+		+	two
+	+	+	+	+
	+	ten	+	

→ = fifteen   ↓ = fifteen   ↘ = fifteen

The living world

Colours

1 Find the right fish in the aquarium. Write the numbers.

■ black ___	■ green ___	□ white ___
■ blue ___	■ orange ___	□ yellow ___
■ brown ___	■ red ___	

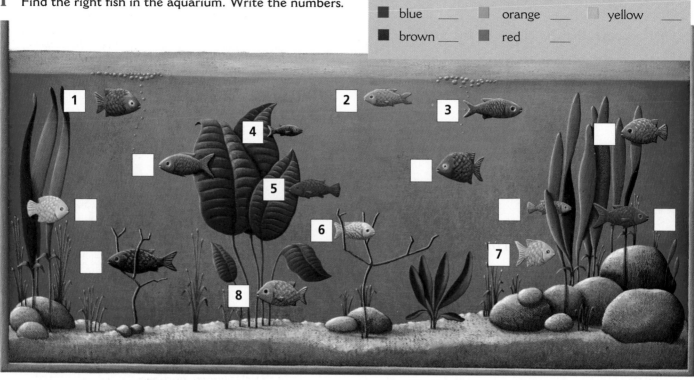

2 a 📼 Listen and repeat the colours.

   b 📼 Listen. One fish is missing on the cassette. What colour is it?

have got

1 📼 Listen and write the numbers nine to fifteen in the boxes next to the other fish.

2 📖 Read 'My pets'. Are the sentences true (✓) or false (✗)? Write ✓ or ✗.

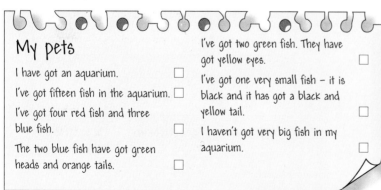

My pets

I have got an aquarium. ☐

I've got fifteen fish in the aquarium. ☐

I've got four red fish and three blue fish. ☐

The two blue fish have got green heads and orange tails. ☐

I've got two green fish. They have got yellow eyes. ☐

I've got one very small fish – it is black and it has got a black and yellow tail. ☐

I haven't got very big fish in my aquarium. ☐

Work it out: *have got* (1)

3 a Underline sentences with *have got* in the text.

   b Complete this chart. Look at the sentences in 'My pets' again.

Positive	Negative
I _____ _____	I haven't got
You have got	You _____ _____
It _____ _____	It _____ _____
We _____ _____	We haven't got
They _____ _____	They _____ _____

4 Read the texts. Match them with two of the pictures. Do not use a dictionary.

The Arctic fox (Picture ___)
The Arctic fox is from the countries in the north of Europe, Asia and North America. In winter this animal is white or grey but in summer it is brown. It has got a small head with short ears, a short nose and black eyes.

The tree frog (Picture ___)
The Central American tree frog is green – the colour of the trees of the Central American forests – but it's got big red eyes, a big mouth and long, yellow and green legs.

Vocabulary: parts of the body

5 Read the texts and look at the pictures again.

a Tick (✓) six words for parts of the body. Do not use a dictionary.

big ☐   ears ☐   eyes ☐   head ☐   legs ☐
long ☐   mouth ☐   nose ☐   short ☐   small ☐

b Now use your dictionary. Check your answers.

6 Match this text with one of the pictures. Complete it with four words from the box.

| colours | ears | Europe | grey | tail | summer |

The glass lizard (Picture ___)

This is not a snake. It is a lizard. It is from _____.

It's got no legs and no _____. It's got a long _____.

The glass lizard is _____ and brown.

7 a ✏ Write a short description of another picture but do not write the animal's name. Use some of these words.

| arms | body | brown | eyes | head | legs | long | neck | small |

b 💬 Work with a partner. Swap your descriptions. Look at the pictures on page 110 and find the name of the animal.

c Write the words for parts of the body on page 73 of the Workbook.

Work it out: plural nouns

8 a Look at Exercise 4. Find the plurals.

Example
eye   _eyes_

1 ear _____   3 leg _____
2 forest _____   4 country _____

b How do you usually make plurals in English? How do you usually make plurals when a word ends in – *y*?

c Complete the table.

1	_an_	eye	two	_____
2	_____	bird	five	_____
3	_____	family	three	_____
4	_____	insect	four	_____

Families

1
Look at the picture of Diana King and her family. Check the words in a dictionary.

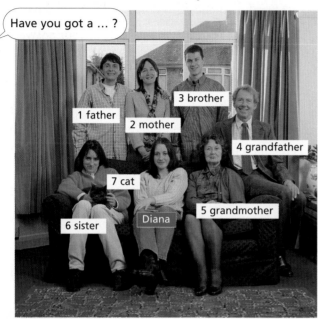

Have you got a ... ?

1 father
2 mother
3 brother
4 grandfather
5 grandmother
6 sister
7 cat
Diana

2
a 📼 Listen. Who's who in the photo? Write the numbers.

David ☐ Hanna ☐ John ☐ Monica ☐
Shakespeare ☐ Sonia ☐ William ☐

b Listen again. Check your answers.

3
Complete this family tree for Diana.

_____ + _____ grandfather
Hanna   _____

_____ + _____
_____   David

_____   Diana   _____
_____   _____

Work it out: *have got* (2)

4
a Make the questions.

You've got a brother.

_____ _____ _____ a brother?

And you've got a sister.

And _____ _____ _____ a sister?

b Put these words in the right order to make questions.

1 you/red pen/?/got/a/Have

2 a/she/?/Has/grandmother/got

3 tail/got/long/a/?/Has/it

5
Answer these questions about the King family. Choose answers from the box.

Yes, he has.   No, he hasn't.
Yes, she has.   No, she hasn't.
Yes, they have.   No, they haven't.

1 Has Diana got a grandfather?
2 Has she got a grandmother?
3 Has her grandmother got white hair?
4 Has her father got a moustache?
5 Has her sister got long hair?
6 Have the Kings got a cat?
7 Have they got a dog?

Pronunciation: *have*

6
a 📼 Listen. Is the pronunciation of *have* the same in the questions as in the short answers? Write *S* (same) or *D* (different).

1 _D_   2 ____   3 ____   4 ____   5 ____

b 📼 Listen and repeat the questions.

c 💬 Work with a partner. Ask and answer the questions in Exercise 5.

d Listen and answer the questions about yourself.
Yes, I have or *No, I haven't*.

A a B b C c D d E e F f G g H h I i J j K k L l M m

7 a Draw your family tree. Look at Diana's family tree again.

b Work with a partner. Ask and answer about your families. Ask about:

your brothers or sisters   your mother and father
your grandparents   pets in your family

Give short answers.

Describing people

1 🔊 Listen. Who are Dan and Tony?

> I don't know Dan. What's he like?

Useful English 🔊

What's she like?	She's got straight, fair hair …
What's he like?	He's got curly, dark hair …

2 💬 Work with a partner. Ask and answer about his/her family tree. Add new information.

A You've got one brother – how old is he?
B He's seventeen.
A What's he like?
B He's got …

3 ✏️ Write a description of yourself for a letter to a penfriend. Brainstorm for ideas. Use these questions.

How old are you?
Are you tall or short?
What colour hair have you got?
Is your hair long or short?
What colour are your eyes?
Are your eyes big or small?

Pronunciation: /eɪ/ and /aɪ/

4 a 🔊 Listen and repeat.

b 💬 Work with a partner.

A Say these words: *he, head, hi, eat, eye, read, red, write, game, these, friend, they.*
B Listen and point to the right word.

c 🔊 Listen and repeat these letters.

A, H, J, K, and I, Y.

d Say these letters:

ID   *BA*   IBM
LA   **DIY**   ICI   *JFK*

e 💬 Work with a partner. Play a game: messages.

A Spell the letters of message 1 for B.
B Close your book. Write the message. Then find message 2 and spell it for A.

Message 1:
P–L–E–A–S–E–G–I–V–E–M–E–A–P–E–N–C–I–L

F–I–N–D–A–B–L–A–C–K–P–E–N–I–N–M–Y–B–A–G
Message 2:

N n O o P p Q q R r S s T t U u V v W w X x **Y y** Z z   23

What a mess!

1 📼 Listen and read. Which of these things do they talk about?

1 paint   2 coffee   3 hair   4 money

2 📖 Read the story. Answer these questions. Who ...

1   ... has got no money?
2   ... has got an idea?
3   ... has only got twenty pence?
4   ... has got 'a fantastic brain'?

1

> **Jane**   Oh, thanks, Dave!
> **Dave**   That's OK.
> **Emma**   Look at the Coffee Corner now!
> **Jack**   What a mess!

2

> **Jane**   You know, I think we're lucky – the old blue and grey paint in this place is awful. Now we've got the chance to change it! Yellow walls, maybe?
> **Jack**   Yes, great idea, Jane, but have we got any money for the paint?
> **Jane**   Er ... no, we haven't.
> **Jack**   So we've got a problem – right?

3

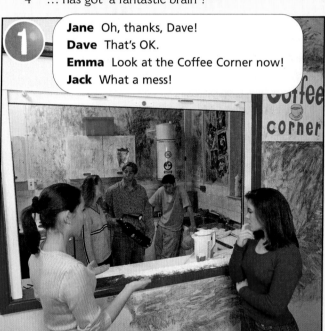

> **Ricky**   I've only got £1.15.
> **Dave**   I haven't got a penny. Carol's got 20p.
> **Jack**   Well, no money – no paint.
> **Jane**   Any ideas?
> **Carol**   No, not really ...

4

> **Ricky**   Look at Emma – her fantastic brain is at work on the problem!
> **Emma**   Yes, I've got an idea. Listen ...

24

3 What is Emma's idea? Guess and explain in your language.

4 a 🗣 Work with a partner. What's the problem? Look at the picture and complete this dialogue.

A Have we _____ any money for the bus?

B I'____ only got _____.

A And I _____ _____ a penny.

B Any ideas?

A Er ... no, not really.

B So we _____ got any money and we haven't _____ any _____!

b Change partners. Practise the dialogue with your new partner.

Review

have got

Positive	Negative
I've got ...	I haven't got ...
You've got ...	You haven't got ...
She/He's got ...	She/He hasn't got ...
It's got ...	It hasn't got ...
We've got ...	We haven't got ...
They've got ...	They haven't got ...
Questions	Short answers
Have I got ... ?	Yes, you have. /No, you haven't.
Have you got ...?	Yes, I have. /No, I haven't.
Has she/he got ...?	Yes, she/he has. /No, she/he hasn't.
Has it got ...?	Yes, it has. /No, it hasn't.
Have we got ...?	Yes, we have. /No, we haven't.
Have they got ...?	Yes, they have. /No, they haven't.

Plural nouns

	Singular	Plural
Regular nouns	cat	cats
– y endings (usually)	family	families

Adjectives

The singular and plural forms of adjectives are the same: *one green book, two green books*.

1 Write two sentences to answer each question.
1 What have you got in your schoolbag?
2 What have you got in your classroom?
3 What has your friend got on his/her desk?

2 Look back at the three texts about animals (Exercises 4 and 6, page 21). Find all the plural nouns in the texts and write them in the singular.

Vocabulary

Look at the unit again. Write all the new words for animals, colours, continents, parts of the body, and members of the family in your vocabulary book.

Freewheeling ....

a 📼 Listen to the song. Write a good title for it.

_____

Has she got a message for him? Make a guess!
Has he got a message for her? Yes! Yes! Yes!
Have they got messages in their eyes?
Don't know. Really don't know ...

Hey! Have I got the time for you?
Have you got the time for me?
Have we got the time to dance together?
Have we got the time to dream?

Hey! Has he got the time for her?
Has she got the time for him?
Have they got the time to dance together?
Have they got the time to dream?

b Listen again. Sing the song.

4 At home

there is, there are

1 Look at the photo. What is the text about?

1 clothes   2 a family   3 a house   4 holidays

Learn to learn: using a dictionary (2)

2 Before you read, find these words in your dictionary.

> bathroom   bedroom   cooker   dining-room
> fridge   garage   kitchen   living-room   sofa

Complete word-map 1 on page 74 of the Workbook. Use one of the ideas in Exercise 1 as your 'head-word'.

3 Read this article about a rich man's dream house. Are these sentences true (✓) or false (✗)?

1 The house is next to a lake. ☐
2 There are 150 chairs in the small living-room. ☐
3 There are ten bathrooms for visitors. ☐
4 Bill Gates and his family watch films in the living-room. ☐
5 There's a private swimming pool at the house. ☐

4 Read the text again. Find words with the same meaning as:

1 house or apartment   3 big
2 a very rich person   4 television

A dream home

Bill Gates is a computer millionaire. He has got a very modern house next to Lake Washington in the USA. His home has got 45 rooms and there are computers for all the rooms. There are computers for all the radios, TVs, videos and fridges in the house.

There are two living-rooms in the house: a small one for Bill Gates and his family and a very large one with sofas and chairs for 150 people! There are bedrooms for visitors, and 12 bathrooms. There is a very large kitchen with all the usual things in it: a fridge, a cooker, a table and some chairs.

Bill Gates and his family sometimes watch films in their private cinema – all the films are on computer – or they swim in their private swimming pool. They also have a garage for 20 cars.

Useful English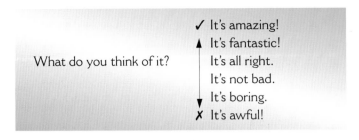

What do you think of it?	✓ It's amazing!
	▲ It's fantastic!
	It's all right.
	It's not bad.
	It's boring.
	✗ It's awful!

5 👥 **Work in a group. What do you think of this dream home? Use some of the 'Useful English' expressions.**

6 📖 **Read this text about the house below. Which room is it: 1, 2, 3 or 4?**

In this room there is a large bed next to the wall and there's an armchair in the corner, next to the window. Next to this room there is a private bathroom with a shower.

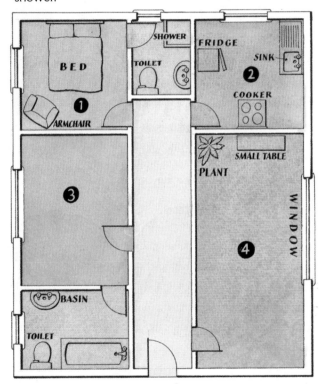

7 📼 **Listen. Draw these things in the right places in the house.**

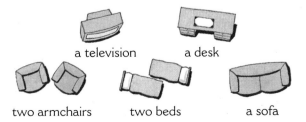

a television a desk

two armchairs two beds a sofa

8 **Write the numbers of the rooms.**

living-room ☐ kitchen ☐

big bedroom (and its private bathroom) ☐

small bedroom (and its private bathroom) ☐

9 👥 **Work with a partner. Play a game.**

In this house there are also two computers:
A Draw two computers on the house plan. Don't show your partner.
B You've got ten questions – find the computers.

Take turns to ask and answer.

B Is there a computer in the kitchen?
A No, there isn't.
B Is there a computer in the big bathroom?
A Yes, there is.
B Is it near the basin?
A Yes, it is – well done!

Work it out: *there is/there are*

10 a 🖊 **Look at the sentences and complete the rules.**

There is a sofa in the living-room.
There are two armchairs in the living-room.

We use _____ _____ with singular nouns.

We use _____ _____ with plural nouns.

b **Write short answers to these questions about the house in Exercise 6.**

1 Is there a shower in the house? _____

_____

2 Are there three toilets in the house? _____

_____

c **How do you make questions with *there is/there are*?**

11 a **Read this description. Put in the capital letters.**

In
in my house there are four rooms. there's a big living-room. in the living-room there are three armchairs. there's a sofa in the corner, near the window.

b 🖊 **Write a description of your home.**

27

Shirts and skirts

Prepositions of place

1 Find these words in a dictionary. Then look at these pictures. Which clothes are in the pictures? Complete word-map 2 on page 74 of the Workbook.

> jeans jumper shirt shoes skirt socks
> T-shirt sweatshirt trainers trousers

Carol's room

Dave's room

2 a 📼 Listen to Carol and Dave's mother. Who is she talking to? Use the pictures to help you.

b 📖 Read this description of the other room. Look at the picture. Find three mistakes in the description.

There are trainers and T-shirts on the chair. There is a ball in the corner and a pair of shoes near the door. There are jeans and sweatshirts on the desk! There's a school bag under the bed, and there are some socks next to it. There's a plant under the desk, too.

in   on   under   next to   near

3 a 🖊 Work with a partner. Choose one room each. Look at it for one minute. Close your book and write five sentences about it.

Example
There's a bag under the bed. There are …

b Check the sentences with your partner.

A Read out one of your sentences.
B Open your book. Listen and check A's sentence. Answer: *Yes, there is/are* or *No, there isn't/aren't.*

Work it out: possessive 's

4 a Look at these pictures.

Jane's book   Ricky's pen   Jack's socks

b Complete these sentences.

This is _____ jumper.   This is _____ T-shirt.

c What is the meaning of *'s* in the sentences?

d 🗣 Work with a partner. Take turns to say a sentence about one of the rooms. Your partner listens and says *It's Dave's room* or *It's Carol's room*.

Example
A *There's a plant on the desk.*
B *It's Carol's room.*

What's your favourite team?

1 📖 Read and match the people and the American football teams.

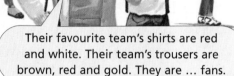

Her team's shirts are blue with red and white numbers. The players have blue helmets with a red 'C' on them. She's a … fan.

4

Your team's colours are red, white and blue. The trousers are white with some red and the socks are red. You're a … fan.

1

2

3

Our team's shirts and trousers are red, gold and blue. Our helmets are gold with a red and blue 'M' on them. We're in the …

My favourite player is Andy Kowolski. His shirt is green and white. His trousers and socks are white, blue and red. He's in the …

5

Their favourite team's shirts are red and white. Their team's trousers are brown, red and gold. They are … fans.

London Monarchs

Chicago Bears

Barcelona Dragons

San Francisco 49ers

Denver Broncos

Work it out: possessive adjectives

2 a Complete the chart. Use Exercise 1 to help you.

I've			my	
You've			____	
He's	got a TV.	It's	____	TV.
She's			____	
We've			____	
They've			____	

b Write sentences with the possessive adjectives.

Example
He's got blue and red socks. *His socks are blue and red.*

1 We've got white trousers.
2 You've got blue and red socks.
3 She's got a red and white skirt.
4 I've got a green and white football shirt.
5 They've got gold helmets.

c Add new words for clothes to the word-map in your Workbook.

Pronunciation: /uː/, /ɑː/ and /əʊ/

3 a 📼 Listen and repeat these letters.

Q, U, W, R, O

b 💬 Work with a partner. Spell these words.

word   door   room   who   quick

c 📼 You can now say all the letters of the English alphabet. Listen and repeat all the letters from A to Z.

Emma's idea

THE OK CLUB

1 a What is Emma's idea? Look at pictures 1 and 2 and guess. Explain it in your language.

b 📼 Listen and read. Check your guess.

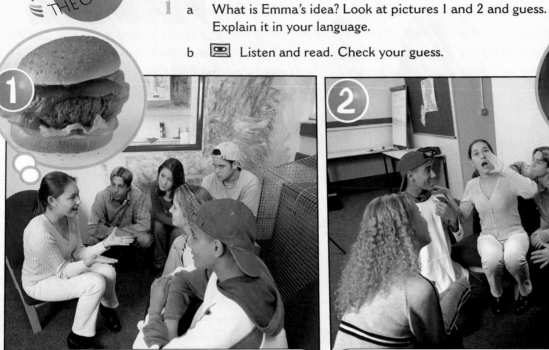

Emma Right. Here's my idea. Let's sell hamburgers outside the OK Club on Saturday. Then all the money from the hamburgers is for 'Project OK' – for our work on the Coffee Corner...

Emma Ricky's got a loud voice. He's in the street, see?
Ricky Yes, listen. 'The OK is not OK! Buy an OK hamburger – save the OK Club!'
Carol That's fantastic, Ricky!

Jane Yes! Right! Who's for Emma's plan? Hands up! ... Jack? Not you?
Jack Er... Sorry, no. Not me. I've ... er ... got a date with ... er ... with a friend in town on Saturday.

What's wrong with *him*?

A date? Who with?

It's an excuse. He's not happy about Jane and Dave.

Jane Bye! See you tomorrow, Dave.
Dave Yes. See you, Jane.
Carol _____ you!
Emma _____ night!

2 Complete Carol's and Emma's words in picture 5.

3 a What do you think these words mean? Guess.

   1 a loud voice   2 a date   3 an excuse

   b Check your guesses in a dictionary.

Set the pace

4 a What is another word or phrase for:

   1 See?   2 Fantastic!   3 See you, Jane.

   b 📼 Listen and repeat.

   c Work in groups. Act out the dialogue.

5 One word in these sentences is wrong. Change it and write the sentences again.

   Example
   Emma has got an ~~awful~~ idea.
   Emma has got a fantastic idea.

   1 Ricky has got a boring voice.
   2 Carol thinks that Emma's idea is awful.
   3 Jack has got a date with a doctor on Saturday.

6 What do you think of Emma's plan?

Review

there is/there are

Statements	Questions	Answers
There is … (There's)	Is there …?	Yes, there is./ No, there isn't.
There are …	Are there …?	Yes, there are./ No, there aren't.

Use *there is* … (+ singular noun) or *there are* … (+ plural noun) to talk about the place or position of things.
There is a red shirt on the chair.
There are two jumpers on the bed.

Prepositions of place

Use prepositions of place to talk about the position of things.

'Where's my jumper?' 'It's in/on/near/under/next to your chair.'

Possessive *'s*

Add *'s* to a singular noun or name to show possession: *This is Bill's new house.* (This is *his* new house.) *This is Emma's mother.* (This is *her* mother.)

1 Complete the sentences with *is/isn't* or *are/aren't*.

   1 There _____ two bedrooms.
   2 There _____ a large living-room.
   3 There _____ three bedrooms – only two.
   4 There _____ a bath in the bathroom – only a shower.

2 Match the words with the pictures. Don't look at page 28 again.

   next to _____   under _____   in _____
   on _____   near _____

   1 2 3 4 5

3 🖊 Work with a partner. Look back at the house on page 27.

   A Write three questions about the things in the house with the question word *Where?*

   Example
   Where's the cooker?

   B Write answers to your partner's questions.

Vocabulary

Look back at the unit. Write all the new words for rooms, furniture, clothes and adjectives on pages 74 and 75 of the Workbook.

Freewheeling ....

Complete the words in the puzzle.

THE CLOTHES PUZZLE

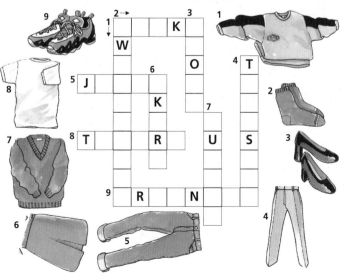

The best of British

The present simple

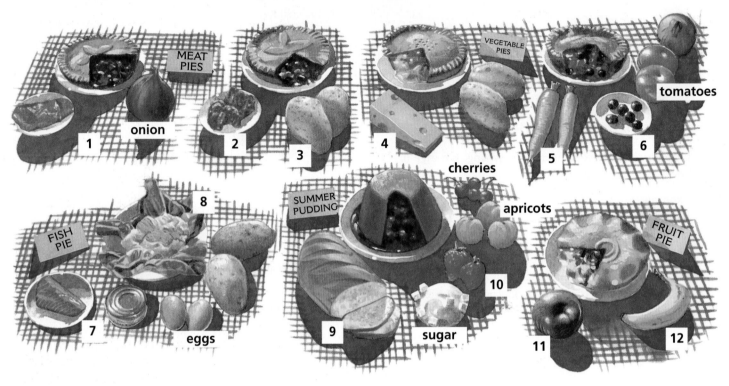

Vocabulary: food

1 a Look at the picture. Match the words to the ingredients. Use a dictionary to help you.

apple	*11*	carrots	—	olives	—
banana	—	cheese	—	potatoes	—
beef	*1*	lamb	—	strawberries	—
bread	—	lettuce	—	tuna	—

  b Start a family tree of new words on page 76 of the Workbook or in your vocabulary book.

2 🔲 Listen. Are these sentences true (✓) or false (✗)?

1 They don't eat a lot of meat. ☐

  They like vegetables and they like olives. ☐

2 They like fish pie. ☐

  They don't like cheese and potato pie. ☐

Work it out: the present simple (1)

3 a Complete the verb chart.

	Positive	Negative
I/You We/They	like eat	_____ _____

Questions	Short answers
Do you like … ? they eat … ?	Yes, I/we do. No, I/we don't.

  b Answer the questions:
  Yes, I do or *No, I don't.*

  1 Do you like pies?   3 Do you like fruit?
  2 Do you like fish?   4 Do you like vegetables?

4 🗣 Work with a partner. Ask and answer about some of the things in the picture of the pies.

  A Do you eat a lot of potatoes?
  B Yes, I do./No, I don't.

5 📖 Read the text. Choose the best title.

1 The secret of Indian spices
2 Britain's favourite food
3 The story of British cooking

British food? Do you think of roast beef or fish and chips or a meat pie? Yes, British people eat these things but they also like international food. In London, for example, there are hundreds of Chinese, Italian and French restaurants – and there are thousands of Indian restaurants.

British people love hot, spicy Indian food. Some people enjoy cooking it at home.

Madhur Jaffrey is a famous Indian cook in Britain. She teaches people about Indian cooking in her TV programmes and recipe books. Her Indian dishes use lamb, chicken, fish, vegetables and rice. She doesn't use a lot of pork or beef in the recipes because some Indian people don't eat pigs or cows.

The secret of Indian cooking is in the ingredients. Some important ingredients in Indian cooking are:

onions and garlic

coriander

chillies and spices

oil and salt

6 Read the text again. Find the names of:

1 three British meals.
2 three different sorts of restaurant in London.
3 British people's favourite sort of food.
4 a book about cooking.
5 three important ingredients in Indian cooking.

Work it out: the present simple (2)

7 **a** Look at the text again. Complete the chart.

Positive	Negative
He uses …	He **doesn't** use …
She cooks …	She _____ cook …
It makes …	It _____ make …

Questions	Short answers
Does he use …?	Yes, he does/ No, he doesn't.
_____ she cook …?	Yes, she _____/ No, she _____.
_____ it make …?	Yes, it _____/ No, it _____.

b Answer these questions: *Yes, she does* or *No, she doesn't.*

1 Does Madhur Jaffrey use chicken in some of her dishes?
2 Does she make dishes with beef?
3 Does she cook with onions and other vegetables?
4 Does she write about British cooking in her books?
5 Does she use spicy ingredients in her cooking?

8 🗫 Work with a partner. Ask and answer about the food in your families. Take turns.

A Who is the main cook in your family?
B My mother/My sister/My father.
A What dishes does she/he make?
B She/He makes a lot of dishes with rice/meat/fish and we eat a lot of …
A What things does she/he use in her/his cooking?
B She/He uses beef and …

Pronunciation: /s/, /z/, and /ɪz/

9 **a** 📼 Listen. Write the words in the right list – look at the examples.

1 /s/: *eats*, _____, _____, _____, _____
2 /z/: *buys*, _____, _____
3 /ɪz/: *uses*, _____

b Listen and repeat.

What would you like?

Ordering food

1 📖 Read the menu. Find the names of two different sorts of:
1 spicy pizza   2 thin pizza

2 📼 Listen. What do these people want?

1 Shannon wants _____

2 Kerry wants _____

3 Steve wants _____

3 Listen again. Complete the dialogue.

Steve   Right, Shannon. What _____ _____ _____?

Shannon   I_____ _____ a _____ pizza.

Steve   OK, – an _____ pizza?

Shannon   Yes, I_____ _____ an _____ pizza, please … and some extra _____, too, please.

Useful English 📼

> Would you like an American pizza? Yes, please.
> Would you like some lemonade? No, thank you.
> I'd like some water, please. Me too! Thank you.

4 🗣 Work with a partner. Make your own dialogue. Then practise it.

Work it out: countable and uncountable nouns

5 a Look at the countable and uncountable nouns.

Countable	Uncountable
an egg	some bread
two eggs	some rice

b Look at the 'extras' again. Write them in two lists, countable nouns and uncountable nouns.

6 🗣 Work in a group. Order pizzas from the menu. Take turns to be the waiter.

THE INTERNATIONAL
PIZZA CAFE
◆
Try one of our delicious pizzas from round the world.

ITALIAN - A big but very thin pizza with tomato sauce, mushrooms and cheese. Choose two other things from our list of extras!

£5.50

AMERICAN - A big, thick pizza with tomatoes, mushrooms … and three extras from our list – you choose!

£6.30

MEDITERRANEAN - A spicy pizza with beef or sausage and onions. Choose olives or extra cheese from our list of extras.

£7.40

MEXICAN - A delicious thin pizza with a very spicy tomato and onion sauce on it. Choose meat or chicken from our list of extras and make a meal of it!

£7.60

◆

EXTRAS

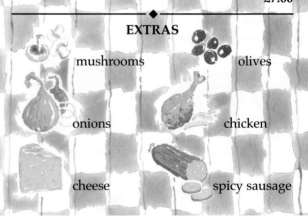

mushrooms   olives

onions   chicken

cheese   spicy sausage

Pronunciation: numbers 21-100

7 a 📼 Listen and repeat the prices.

30p 40p 50p 60p 70p 80p 90p 100p (£1)
55 cents   95 cents   100 cents (€1)

b 📼 Listen and repeat the numbers.

21 22 23 24 25 26 27 28 29 30 31 …

c 📼 Listen. Which is the right price?

1 Steve wants £5.15/£5.50.
2 That's €6.13/€6.30.
3 A Mexican pizza with extra meat is £7.16/£7.60.

some and any

1 📖 Read and match the names and the drinks. Use your dictionary. Write the missing names.

DRINKS

Cold drinks

Milk large £1.25
    small 99p
Cola large 85p
    small 75p

Mineral water 85p
Orange juice £1.15
Lemonade large 85p
    small 75p

Hot drinks

Coffee with milk 99p
Black coffee 95p

Hot chocolate 95p
Tea 60p

Milkshakes

Banana Chocolate Coffee Vanilla £1.35

1 ___ 2 ___ 3 ___ 4 ___ 5 ___
6 ___ 7 ___ 8 ___ 9 ___ 10 ___ 11 ___ 12 ___

2 ▣ Listen to the people at the Pizza Cafe. What do they want?

3 Complete the sentences about the people.

1 She wants a _____ with some _____. She doesn't want any _____.

2 She wants a _____ milkshake. She doesn't want any _____ _____.

3 She wants a _____ _____ with some _____.

4 The waiter asks, 'Would you like _____ sugar?'

Work it out: *some* and *any*

4 a Complete these rules.

We usually use _____ in positive sentences.

We usually use _____ in questions.

We usually use _____ in negative sentences.

b 🗪 Work with a partner. Take turns.

  A You are the customer. Choose some food and a drink from the menu and order it: *I'd like …*

  B You are the waiter. Write the order. Ask: *Would you like …?*

5 🗪 Work with a partner. *Have you got any …?*

  A Turn to page 110. Answer B's questions.

  B You are a customer in a shop. Look at your shopping list. Ask A *I'd like some …/six … Have you got any …?* Tick (✓) or cross (✗) the things on your list.

> *white bread*
> *6 eggs*
> *4 large tomatoes*
> *cheese*
> *8 large potatoes*
> *rice*

'Make a drink' competition

6 a Read the description.

> My drink for the competition has got some yoghurt and milk in it. It's got three bananas and some sugar. It hasn't got any water in it, but it's got some ice.

b Make a drink for the competition. From the box, choose the things you want in your drink.

> carrot juice cherry juice cola fruit juice
> hot chocolate lemon juice milk tomato juice
> vegetable juice water
> with …
> bananas cheese chocolate coffee coriander
> eggs garlic ice Indian spices ice cream salt
> sugar yoghurt

c Make a word-map of the things in your drink. Write the name of your drink in the centre.

d ✎ Write a description of your drink.

Hamburgers

1 📼 Listen and read. What are these things? Write the words for them.

1 _____ 2 _____ 3 _____ 4 _____

1 **Saturday**

Do you want to help the OK Club? OK! Come on! Come and have a hamburger! Only £1.55!

Emma Do you want onions?
Boy No, thanks. But I'd like some extra ketchup, please.
Emma That's £1.55, please.
Mother No mustard, please. She doesn't like mustard.

2 **Jack is at work.**

Mmm, I like Harleys. They're fantastic bikes.

3 **Later, at the club**

Ricky We've got £62! That's really good!
Jack And here's another £16. It's from my work today at my brother's garage.
Dave Your what? Your work …?
Jane That's great, Jack!
Ricky Fantastic! Now we've got £78!

4

Carol Look, Dave. There's a man and a woman at the door. _____ are they? _____ do they _____ ?

2 Complete Carol's words in picture 4 of the story.

3 What do the man and the woman want? Who are they? Make a guess.

4 a Answer these questions with full sentences.
   1 Who wants extra ketchup?
   2 Who doesn't want any onions?
   3 Who doesn't want any mustard?
   4 Who likes Harley Davidson bikes?

   b And you? Do you like …
   1 hamburgers?   3 mustard?
   2 ketchup?   4 onions?

   Write short answers.

Review

The present simple tense (*like, eat* …)

Positive	Negative
I/you like …	I/you don't like …
He/She likes …	He/She doesn't like …
We/They like …	We/They don't like …
Questions	
Do you like …? Does he/she like …? Do we/they like …?	

Countable and uncountable nouns

Countable nouns – things we count.
pen: one pen, two pens, three pens …
Uncountable nouns – things we don't count.
milk: some milk

some and *any*

We usually use *some*:
- with countable and
  uncountable nouns   *some cars   some water*
- in positive sentences   *I'd like some information.*

We usually use *any*:
- in questions   *Do you want any ketchup?*
- in negative sentences   *I don't want any onions.*

1 Write a complete verb table for two more verbs: *want* and *use*.

2 👓 Work with other students in the class.

   a Write two lists of three things. Do not show your lists to other students.

List 1	List 2
I like …	*I don't like …*

   b Ask and answer with other students. Find other people with the same things in their lists.

   c What do/don't other students like? Write five sentences.

3 Look again at the six things on your lists. Are the nouns countable or uncountable? Write *C* (for countable nouns) or *U* (for uncountable nouns) next to them in the lists.

4 Write about two things you want and two things you don't want for your birthday. Use *some* or *any* in your sentences.

   Example
   I don't want any books. I want some new CDs.

Vocabulary

Look at the unit again. Add all the new food and drink and nationality words from this unit to pages 75 and 76 of the Workbook.

Freewheeling ....

Look at the list of prices in the fruit shop and work out the puzzle.

Prices puzzle

1 What does a lemon cost?   2 What does a pear cost?
Clue: think about the number of letters.

TODAY ONLY! SPECIAL PRICES!
An apple costs only 25 pence!
A banana costs only 30 pence!
An orange costs only 30 pence!
A coconut costs only 35 pence!

Compare your answers with other students.

Consolidation

Grammar

1 Look at the pictures. Complete the dialogues.

1

Hi! I'm Kevin. I'm ¹ _____ London.

Hello. ² _____ Tina, from Brazil.

³ _____ this? It's my friend, Sara.

He's my boyfriend.

⁴ _____ nice. And who's that?

Oh.

2

⁵ _____ you like a sausage pizza?

No, thanks, Kevin.

Well, would you ⁶ _____ an ice cream?

No, thanks, Kevin.

Do you ⁷ _____ pizza and ice cream?

Yes, I ⁸ _____, but Kevin, I don't want to eat them here in the street with you!

3

This is our house. It's ⁹ _____ four bedrooms. I've got a really big bedroom and I ¹⁰ _____ got a great new TV!

Wow! Is that ¹¹ _____ house, Jim? ¹² _____ has got a swimming pool!

Yes, and it ¹³ _____ got eight bedrooms, three living-rooms, and a games room.

2 Complete the questions and answers about the pictures.

1 *Where's* Kevin *from?* He's from _____ .

2 _____ _____ Kevin _____ ?
   He likes _____ pizza and _____ _____ .

3 What _____ Kevin _____ in his bedroom?
   He's got a _____ .

4 _____ Jim _____ a games room?
   Yes, _____ _____ .

3 a Write the names of these things in the correct list.

Countable	Uncountable
mushroom	ice cream

b 🗣 Work with a partner. Write six food words from the lists. Take turns to ask and answer.

A Ask for one thing from your words. *I'd like some ..., please.*

B Answer. Use your list. *Here you are./Sorry, I haven't got any ...*

Vocabulary

1 Find the words. They are all about homes, food and drink, clothes or colours.

zapiz onwrb offcee ragega yerg rumpje chikten
totpasoe reshow teaswthirs nerstari lowley

2 Put the words from Exercise 1 into lists.

Clothes	Colours	Food & drink	The home
jumper			

3 a Complete the chart with countries and nationalities. Use a dictionary.

Country	Nationality
Brazil	Brazilian
Britain	British
China	_____
France	_____
_____	Greek
India	_____
_____	Italian
_____	Japanese
Poland	_____
Portugal	Portuguese
_____	Spanish
Turkey	_____
The United States	_____

b Look at the endings in the nationalities. There are three patterns. What are they? Which nationalities are different?

4 Complete the word puzzle with food words. What's the extra word?

```
            P
          T
    L  E  T
    B  R  E
    M
    O
    R
C
```

5 Check your vocabulary book. Have you got all the words from these exercises? Add any new words.

Communication

1 Complete this dialogue with one word for each gap. Make guesses.

Anna	Hello, **Paolo**. _____ are you?
Paolo	Hi, I'm _____, thanks.
Anna	Well, here we are. _____ is my **house**.
Paolo	It's _____!
Anna	Yes. Come in. We're all in the _____-room.
Paolo	Thanks.
Anna	This is my mother. Mum, this is **Paolo**. **He's from Italy**.
Paolo	Hello.
Mum	_____ to meet you, **Paolo**.
Anna	And this is my _____, **Tina**.
Paolo	Hello, **Tina**.
Tina	_____, **Paolo**.
Anna	Where's Dad?
Mum	He's at work. He's _____ a problem with the new **computers**.
Anna	Oh dear!
Mum	Now, **Paolo**, sit down. Would you _____ some **coffee**?
Paolo	Oh, yes, _____.
Mum	Do you want milk and _____?
Paolo	Milk, please, but I don't want _____ sugar, thanks.
Mum	OK, here you are ...

2 📼 Listen. Are your answers the same as the answers on the cassette?

3 🗣 Work with a partner. Make a new dialogue. Change the words in **bold**.

Project: a letter to a penfriend
Reading

1 This is a letter from Carol to her new penfriend. What do you think she writes about? Tick three boxes.

her family ☐ her clothes ☐ her pets ☐
her home ☐ her school ☐ pop stars ☐

2 📖 Read the letter and check your answers.

3 Draw a family tree for Carol and her family. Put names and ages on it.

57 Merton Road
Oxford
OX8 1EX
England
3rd May

1 Dear

Hello! I'm Carol and I'm your new penfriend. I'm fourteen years old and I'm a student. I'm short and I've got brown hair and blue eyes.

2 I live in a small house in Oxford with my parents and my brother. My father is a cook and my mother's a teacher. She's called Anna and my father's name is Roger. My brother, Dave, is sixteen and he's a student, too. He's in the photo of my family.

3 Our house is very nice. We've got three bedrooms. I've got a bedroom and Dave's got a bedroom. We've got a living-room and a large kitchen. We haven't got a garage, but we've got a small garden.

4 I like pop music and football; yes, really! I don't like TV or computers, but I really like animals. We've got two black-and-white cats, called Ralph and Spike, and we've got five birds.

5 Please write to me and tell me about you.
Yours,
Carol

4 Correct these mistakes.

Example
Carol's tall and she's got short fair hair.
No, she isn't tall. She's short. She hasn't got short
fair hair. She's got long brown hair.

1 Carol's mother is called Anna. She's a doctor.
2 Carol's got a brother and sister.
3 There are four bedrooms in Carol's house.
4 Carol likes TV and computers.

Listening

5 🔊 Carol's penfriend has got the letter. Listen to the conversation with her mother. Is she a good penfriend for Carol?

6 a Listen again. Complete the chart.

	likes	doesn't like
Carol		
her penfriend		

b Find two differences and write sentences.
Carol likes _____ but her penfriend likes _____.

Before you write

7 Match the paragraphs in the letter with these topics.

Topic	Paragraph
her home	_____
what she likes/doesn't like	_____
her family	_____
a description of herself	_____

8 Look at this information about Carol. Complete the notes.

Name: Carol Hill
Age: _____ years old
Description: short; long brown hair, blue eyes
       Family: mother, father, _____
Home: big/small? small
       number of bedrooms _____
       garage? no   garden? _____
Likes: pop music, football, _____
Doesn't like: TV, _____

9 Complete this information about yourself.

Name: _____
Age: _____
Description: _____
Family: _____
Home: big/small?
       number of bedrooms _____
       garage? _____   garden? _____
Like: _____
       _____
Don't like: _____
       _____

Writing: a letter to a penfriend

10 a Plan your letter. Look at the information about yourself in Exercise 9. Write the numbers 1, 2, 3 or 4 (for the paragraphs in your letter) next to your notes.

Name: _____David_____ 1

b Find some photos to go with your letter. Put one or two sentences about the photos in your letter.

c Use the information from Exercise 9 to write a letter to Carol. Start like this:

Hello! I'm _____ . Thanks for your letter. I'm _____ years old and I'm _____ . I'm _____, I've got …

d ✏️ Finish the letter. Use Carol's letter to help you.

Check your vocabulary book

Before you start Unit 6 check that all the new words in Units 1-5 are in your vocabulary book.

Life and times

Frequency

1 🎞️ **Listen. Choose the right answers.**

1 Where are the people in the photo?
   a At home   b In a studio   c At a party
2 Who are they?
   a Dancers   b Musicians   c Actors

2 🎞️ **Listen. Tick the questions you hear.**

1 Do you come from Australia? ☐
2 Do you visit a lot of different places? ☐
3 Do you usually travel in the day or at night? ☐
4 Do you usually travel by plane or by bus? ☐
5 Do you find time for relaxation or exercise? ☐
6 Do you take some exercise every day? ☐
7 Do you start work in the afternoon? ☐

3 Before you listen again, try to complete the group's answers. Then listen and check your answers.

1 Yes we _____ . We always _____ four or five different cities when we're on tour.

2 We often _____ at night … Sometimes we have a tour bus …

3 Me? Exercise? No way! I never take _____ . I usually stay in bed and _____ to the _____ or watch a _____ until about eleven o'clock.

4 Yes we usually _____ work after lunch, at about two o'clock. We often _____ from then to five or six o'clock.

4 Are these sentences true (✓) or false (✗)?

1 The group never travels at night, after a concert. ☐

2 Alex usually goes swimming in the morning. ☐

3 Patty sometimes goes shopping when she is on tour. ☐

4 They often work for three or four hours in the afternoon, before a concert. ☐

5 The group always eats an evening meal before their concert. ☐

Work it out: adverbs of frequency

5 a Look at the sentences in Exercise 4 again. Then look at the diagram. What do the words mean? Explain in your language.

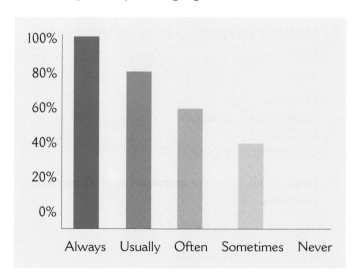

b Look at the chart. Complete these sentences with one of the words.

1 Alex _____ goes swimming in the morning. (80%)
2 She _____ eats breakfast. (0%)
3 She _____ watches TV in the morning. (100%)
4 She _____ writes letters in the evening. (40%)
5 She _____ uses a computer in the studio. (60%)

6  Work with a partner. Ask and answer questions about a singer's life on tour. Take turns to be the singer.

A Do you often travel by plane/go shopping/visit interesting places/watch videos or TV?

B Yes, I/we do./No, we don't. I/We always/usually/sometimes/never …

Telling the time

What time is it, please?

It's two o'clock.

1 a Look at the times on these clocks.

To Past

It's **quarter past** one.

It's **half past** two.

It's **quarter to** three.

It's ten **past** four.

It's twenty **past** six.

It's twenty-five **to** five.

It's five **to** eight.

b 📼 Listen and repeat the times.

c 📼 Listen. Draw clocks with the right times.

d What time is it now? It's _____

2 Survey. Complete the chart with true answers about your habits. Write the percentages.

This Is Your Life

always = 100%	usually = about 80%	often = about 60%
sometimes = about 40%	never = 0%	

	Your name	Your partner's name
1 I arrive at school before eight o'clock in the morning.	_____	_____
2 I go to a club after school in the afternoon.	_____	_____
3 I take some exercise after school.	_____	_____
4 I do my homework in the morning, before school.	_____	_____
5 I watch TV in the evening.	_____	_____
6 I read the newspaper or a book in the evening.	_____	_____
7 I go to bed after ten o'clock.	_____	_____
8 I meet my friends at the weekend.	_____	_____

Useful English 📼

in the morning   in the afternoon   in the evening
at night   at the weekend

3 a  Work with a partner. Ask and answer questions. Complete the chart for your partner.

A Do you go to bed after ten o'clock at night?

B Yes, I sometimes go to bed after ten o'clock.

b Work with a different partner. Ask your new partner about his/her first partner.

A Does Magda arrive at school before eight o'clock?

B No, she never arrives before eight. She's usually late!

4 ✏️ Write a paragraph about your new partner.

Carnival time

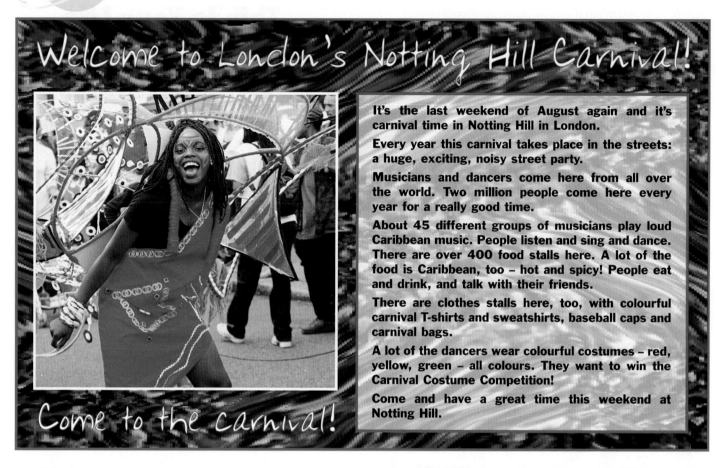

Welcome to London's Notting Hill Carnival!

It's the last weekend of August again and it's carnival time in Notting Hill in London.

Every year this carnival takes place in the streets: a huge, exciting, noisy street party.

Musicians and dancers come here from all over the world. Two million people come here every year for a really good time.

About 45 different groups of musicians play loud Caribbean music. People listen and sing and dance. There are over 400 food stalls here. A lot of the food is Caribbean, too – hot and spicy! People eat and drink, and talk with their friends.

There are clothes stalls here, too, with colourful carnival T-shirts and sweatshirts, baseball caps and carnival bags.

A lot of the dancers wear colourful costumes – red, yellow, green – all colours. They want to win the Carnival Costume Competition!

Come and have a great time this weekend at Notting Hill.

Come to the carnival!

1 🔊 Listen to the carnival music. What sort of music do you have at a carnival or a party?

2 📖 Read the text quickly. Choose a title for the photo.

1 Singers in the street
2 Dancers at the carnival
3 London's great street party

3 Read the text again. Find a word or phrase which means the same as:

1 carnival   3 loud
2 very big   4 colourful clothes for a special party

4 Read the text again. Write short answers to these questions.

1 When does the carnival take place?
2 Where does it take place?
3 Where do the musicians and dancers at the carnival come from?
4 Where does a lot of the food come from?
5 What do a lot of the dancers wear?

Work it out: the present simple (3)

5 a Complete the two questions.

The dancers wear colourful costumes.	
Do the dancers _____ colourful costumes?	What _____ the dancers _____ ?
This sort of question asks for a Yes or No answer: *Yes, they do.*	This sort of question asks for information: *They wear colourful costumes.*

b Change the five questions in Exercise 4 into *Yes* or *No* questions.

Examples

1 When does the carnival take place?
   Does the carnival take place in August?
2 Where does it take place? *Does it ...?*

Object pronouns

A

Hungry after a long day at the Carnival?
Come and see me at the
Jamaican Jive – **Big John** is my name.
You've got the appetite and I've got the food.
See you there – at the Jamaican Jive.

B

Do you want to dance?

◆ Visit us at ◆

The Dance Studio!
Don't forget your friends
– bring them all with you!
Dance the night away!

◆ **Remember:** ◆

Royston and Rosie,
at the Dance Studio.

C

Does your brother boogie?

Get him some fantastic
Caribbean dance CDs. Get
them only at The Carnival
Club, in the Portobello
Road, London W10.

D

Rosalind Arasis at the International Boutique.

Visit her and see hundreds
of colourful bags from all
round the world!

At the
International Boutique,
243 Cambridge Road.

E

Young, stylish, beautiful!

You can order a designer hat from me for £100 upwards.

Janet Barton,
28 Chelsea Road,
London W10.

1 a  Read these advertisements about the carnival quickly. Which advert is for:

1	a disco? ☐	4	a food stall? ☐
2	a hat shop? ☐	5	a music shop? ☐
3	a bag shop? ☐		

b These words are object pronouns: *me, you, him, her, us, you, them*. Find them in the five adverts and say who these people are.

Advert A	1	you	*the reader*
	2	me	_____
Advert B	3	us	_____
	4	them	_____
Advert C	5	him	_____
Advert D	6	her	_____
Advert E	7	me	_____

Pronunciation: /æ/ and /ʌ/

2 a 🔊 Listen. Write the words with the same sound in the correct column.

bag	bus	cap	club	come	has	hat
h**u**ndreds	j**a**cket	man	n**u**mber	some		

/æ/	/ʌ/
bag	bus

b 🔊 Listen and repeat. Then say the sentence quickly.

Buying and selling

1 a 🔊 Listen to the dialogue and look at the picture. What do the girls want to look at?

b 💬 Work with a partner. Make new dialogues.

A You've got a clothes shop. You've got T-shirts, jackets, and caps. Choose one colour for each sort of clothes.

B You'd like to buy a green jacket, a red T-shirt, and a yellow cap.

Writing: an advert

2 ✐ Imagine that you have got a shop or a stall at the carnival or at a market in your own town. You sell clothes or food. Look at the carnival adverts again. Write an advert for your shop or stall.

a Plan it. Use a dictionary if necessary.

What do you sell? (Make a list of all the things.)
What special things have you got in the shop/stall this week?
What colours are the things in your shop/stall?
What 'special offers' (special prices) have you got this week?

b Write your advert and check the spelling.

c Add a picture or photo for your advert.

The people from TV 4

1 Read the words in the box and then look quickly at the pictures. Which four words are in the story?

computer   concert   costume   interview
loud   musician   programme   shopping
street   TV company

1

TV Producer Who are we? What do we want? We work for a TV company – TV 4.
Cameraman We want to make a programme about young people's clubs.
Ricky So you want to come here and make a programme about the OK Club, right?
TV Producer That's right – but wait! I'd like to interview *you*!

2

Jane That's great, but we've got a problem. Look at our coffee bar. We want to paint the walls.
TV Producer Fine. You paint the walls. We film you and pay for all the paint! What do you think?

3

Dave That's a fantastic idea!
Jane Wow!
Ricky Thanks a lot!

4 The next day

TV Producer What do you do here?
Ricky We sometimes play table tennis or cards after school. I play my guitar and sing.
Emma Yes, Jack sometimes sings too – it's terrible! Some of us use the computer here.

5

TV Producer What about sports? Do you play football, for example?
Jack Yes, I play football at the weekend. There's a sports centre near here. Ricky and I sometimes go swimming there …
Emma Yes, but he's a hopeless swimmer!
Jack You can talk!

2 **a** 🔲 Listen and read the story. Who does what? Match the names and the phrases. Then write sentences.

Example
play cards → members of the club
Some members of the club play cards.

1	play table tennis	
2	make programmes	Jack
3	play football at the weekend	the TV producer and her cameraman
4	go to a sports centre	
5	interview people	members of the club
6	play the guitar and sing	

b Do you do any of these things? What do you do? Where? When? Write five sentences about your life.

Example
I usually talk to my friends after school.

Review

The present simple

Some verbs add *-es* with *he*, *she* and *it*.

He goes to bed ...   He watches TV ...
She goes to bed ...   She watches TV ...
It goes ...

Negative: She doesn't go to bed ...
Questions: Does he watch TV...?

Adverbs of frequency

always, usually, often, sometimes and *never*
Position: 1   usually before the main verb
             2   always after the verb *be* (*am, is, are*).

Telling the time
What time is it?

ten past ten   half past ten   quarter to eleven

Object pronouns
I	→	me	we	→	us
you	→	you	you	→	you
he	→	him	they	→	them
she	→	her		
it	→	it		

1 **a** ✏️ Write three questions about each phrase. Use *Do/Does* ... or question words: *When, What,* or *Where*.

1 go shopping   2 buy clothes   3 watch TV
Do you go shopping for your family?
Where do you go shopping?

b Work with a partner. Write answers to your partner's questions.

2 Answer these questions about your school day.

What time do you ...
1   ... arrive at school?
2   ... start lessons in the morning?
3   ... stop for lunch?
4   ... start afternoon lessons?
5   ... go home after school?

Vocabulary

Look back at the unit. Add all the new music and dance, adverbs of frequency and time words to your vocabulary book.

Freewheeling ....

a Complete the words of this song with words from the box.

b 🔲 Listen to the song. Check your answers.

come   hear   music   street   sugar   summer   water   winter

Any more

1 _____ doesn't sound good
In my ears any more ...
_____ doesn't taste sweet
In my mouth any more, and ...
_____ doesn't wash away
My blues any more ...
Now that I don't see you,
Now that I don't _____ you,
Now that you don't _____ around
To my place any more.

2 _____ isn't sunshine
And blue sky any more, and ...
_____ isn't cold now
With white snow any more, and ...
The rain doesn't run now
Down my _____ any more ...

Imagine this ...

SPACE STATION 66H, ORBIT Q24

1 🗫 Work in groups. Talk about the picture. What do you know about space stations?

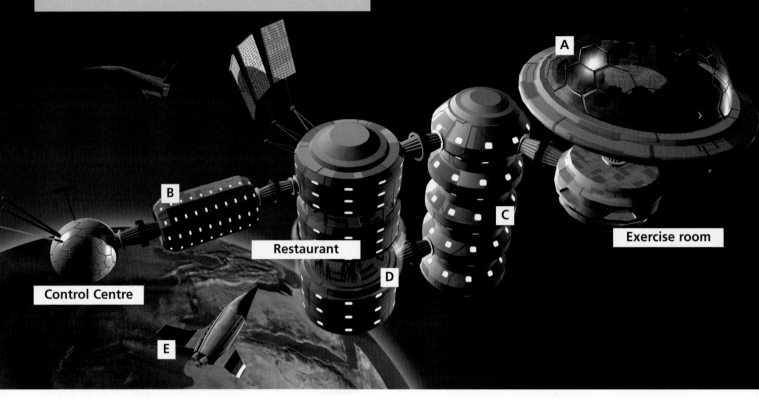

A

B

C **Exercise room**

Restaurant

D

Control Centre

E

2 📖 Read and match the descriptions with parts of the picture. Use a dictionary if necessary. Write A–E in the boxes.

1 Space buses bring people to the space station from Earth. Visitors usually stay for five days. ☐

2 Bedrooms for the visitors are in this part of the station, between the exercise room and the restaurant section. ☐

3 The living-room, restaurant, library and cinema are all in this section of the space station. Visitors sit in the living-room and watch the world go round. ☐

4 This is the Green Area, with its vegetable garden and large play area. The vegetable garden produces salad for the restaurant. ☐

5 The station has a crew of 55 men and women. Their rooms are next to the Control Centre. ☐

3 a 📼 Listen. Which part of the station are these two people in?

b Listen again. Write *that* or *those*.

What's _____?

_____ round thing's Earth, sir. Do you see _____ blue parts? ... _____ are the oceans. ... And _____ black parts are the big cities. _____'s New York.

Really? Isn't it small?

Work it out: *this, that, these* and *those*

4 a Look at these sentences.

What's this room?
These videos and CDs are all here for you.
What's that round thing?
Those blue parts are the oceans.

b Complete the chart. Use *this, that, these* and *those*.

	Singular	Plural
Things near us	_____	_____
Things not near us	_____	_____

Pronunciation: /θ/ and /ð/

5 a 📼 Listen and repeat these words.

thing   this   these   think   there   thanks

b Say the words. Put them in two groups.

1   Words with the same *-th* sound as *thing*.
2   Words with the same *-th* sound as *this*.

c 📼 Listen to the tongue-twister.

There are three things in my brother's brain.
In my brother's brain there are only three things!

d 🗣 Work with a partner. Take turns to say the tongue-twister – quickly!

Describing objects

1 a 📖 Look at the names of the different shapes. Read the descriptions below and find the adjectives for these shapes.

Shape	Noun	Adjective
●	a circle	*1 round 2 circular*
▮	a rectangle	_____
▲	a triangle	_____
■	a square	_____

A is for receiving radio messages and TV pictures from Earth. It is square. It is black, red and green.
B is for sending messages to other space stations. It is triangular. The green balls are radios.
C is round. It is for sending messages to space buses and cargo ships. It is red and black.
D is a computer. It is for receiving information from the crew all over the space station. It is rectangular.

b Read the descriptions again. Find the right pieces of equipment in the picture of the Control Centre. Write A–D in the boxes.

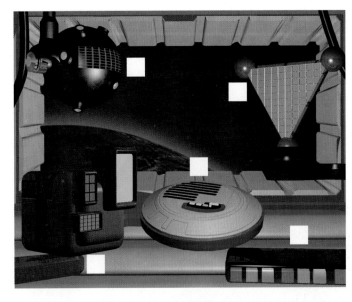

c Write E on the picture. Then complete this description.

E is _____ and thin. It is _____ and grey. It is for sending telephone and videophone messages to Earth.

Useful English 📼

Shape	Purpose
What shape is it?	What's it for?
It's square.	It's for sending messages.
It's round.	It's for receiving messages.
It's circular.	
It's triangular.	What do you do with it?
It's rectangular.	You write messages.

2 📖 Read and guess. What is it?/What are they?

1   They're small and white. They're in your mouth. They're for eating your food! What are they?
2   You put them in socks and also in shoes. They're for walking. What are they?
3   It's round, very large and very hot. The Earth goes round it every year. What is it?

3 ✏️ Work in groups. Write puzzles.

a Think of an object. Don't say what it is. Write two or three sentences about it. What shape or size is it? What colour is it? What's it for?

b Read and answer other people's puzzles.

49

Clever inventions

Quantity

1 Work in groups. What are these inventions for? Talk about them and make guesses.

Example
I think it's for playing music.

2 a Match the pictures with three of the names of these inventions. Write the letters.

1 A space kitchen (on space ships) ☐
2 A message writer ☐
3 A videophone ☐
4 A direction-finder ☐
5 A solar tin-opener ☐

b Compare your guesses with other students' ideas. What are the clues in the pictures?

3 Listen to a scientist. Check your guesses.

4 Listen again. Which of the three inventions do these things? Write A, B or C.

1 It uses only a little electricity. ☐
2 It understands men's and women's voices. ☐
3 It puts a lot of different messages together. ☐
4 It produces a lot of good food. ☐
5 It writes your words on a small screen. ☐
6 It tells you where you are in space. ☐
7 It shows you a few different dishes on a screen. ☐

Work it out: *a little*, *a few* and *a lot of*

5 a Look at the sentences in Exercise 4 again. Tick (✓) the chart.

	a lot of	a little	a few
With uncountable nouns	___	___	___
With countable nouns	___	___	___

b Choose the right phrases to complete these sentences.

1 Scientists make _____ clever inventions. (a little/a lot of)

2 The videophone only uses _____ electricity. (a few/a little)

3 _____ the food and water for the space station comes from Earth. (a lot of/a few)

4 The space kitchen makes _____ Chinese dishes, too. (a little/a few)

5 The space station library has _____ videos in it. (a little/a lot of)

50

In the workshop

1 a Look at the picture of the workshop. Complete the sentences with *a little, a few* or *a lot of.*

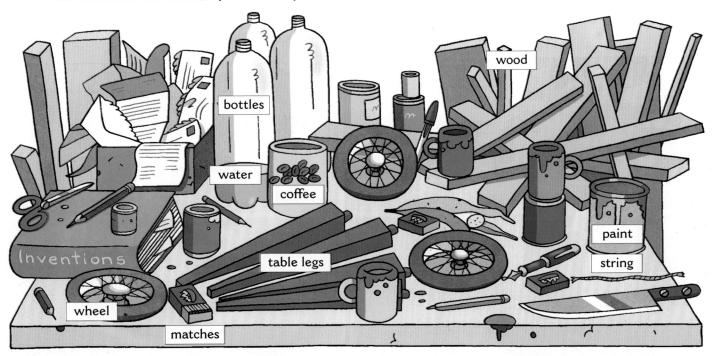

1 There are _____ bottles.

2 There's _____ water in one of the bottles.

3 There are _____ wheels.

4 There's only _____ string.

5 There are _____ boxes of matches.

6 There are _____ tins of paint.

7 There's _____ wood.

8 There are _____ table legs.

b Find the English words for other things in the picture.

2 Work with a partner. Take turns.

A Look at the picture for half a minute. Then close your book. Describe the workshop to B and answer B's questions about the things.

B Check A's statements about the things on the desk. Then ask questions about them.

Examples
'What's in the tins?'
'There is ...'
'Where are the bottles?'
'They're near/behind/in/front of ...'

Writing: an invention

3 Design something useful with the things in the workshop (and any other things you want to use).

Possible inventions: something for your classroom, kitchen, home, garden, your bedroom (for your clothes, books, etc.), a children's toy.

a Work with a partner. Choose one possible invention and talk about your ideas. Make notes of useful vocabulary.

b Plan a description of your invention. Answer these questions.

Who's it for?/What's it for?/What does it do?
What shape and size is it?
Does it move?
Does it use electricity?
Does it have solar panels/a screen/a microphone/wheels or legs?

c Listen to the scientist's description of the direction-finder again.

d Write the description of your invention.

e Draw a picture of your invention. Put the description and the picture together.

Project OK

1 What is 'Project OK' – can you remember?
2 Look at the pictures. What is the story about? Guess.

Thanks, Dave.

Ricky Well. We've now got £178 for painting the Coffee Corner; £78 from our work and £100 from the TV people.
Jack What about brown for the walls?
Jane Brown walls? No way! I'd like yellow …
Dave Yellow – that's a nice, sunny colour! I'd like yellow, too.

Jane I'd like Jack to be the boss for 'Project OK'. What do you all think?
Jack Me? Project boss? … Well, all right. I'd like that.
Ricky Yes, that's a good idea, Jane. Jack's the project boss. Don't lose the money, Jack!

Later, at the club

There! That's a good place for it, I think.

Oh no, there's the box with the money in it! Jack's hopeless. He always forgets things!

Then Emma closes the club and runs after the others …

Never mind! My message about the money is there for them tomorrow morning.

3 🔊 Listen and find the mistakes. Write the correct sentences.

1 Jane wants brown paint for the walls.
2 Jack doesn't think brown paint is a good idea.
3 Emma wants Jack to be the boss of Project OK.
4 Carol forgets to take the money home.
5 Emma finds a message in the Coffee Corner later.
6 Emma forgets about the money and goes home.

Set the pace

4 **a** Look at the pictures again. What do these things mean in your language?

1 No way!   3 Jack's hopeless.
2 Don't lose the money!   4 Never mind!

b 🔊 Listen and repeat.

Review

this, *that*, *these* and *those*

This page

These two pages

That bottle

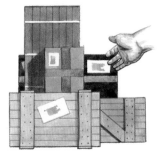

Those boxes

Quantity

A lot of + countable or uncountable nouns: *a lot of water, a lot of visitors*

A little + uncountable nouns only: *a little water*

A few + countable nouns only: *a few visitors*

1 Describe all the things in the diagram. Use *this* or *these* for the things near you and *that* or *those* for the things not near you.

Example
This circle is green.

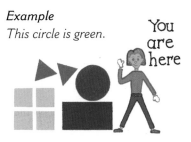

2 Look at the nouns in the box.

a Put them in two lists, countable and uncountable.

> children   electricity   feet   ideas   knives
> legs   men   paint   people   string   teeth
> water   women   wood   work

b Choose two countable nouns and two uncountable nouns. Write true sentences with the nouns and *a lot of*, *a little* or *a few*.

Example
water – There is only a little water in this glass.
or *There is a lot of water in my bottle.*

c Find six irregular plural nouns in the box. Start a list of them in your vocabulary book.

Vocabulary

Look at the unit again for space travel, shapes, and useful things at home or at work. Add all the new words to your vocabulary book in word-maps, lists or picture pages.

Freewheeling ·······························

🔊 Listen to this poem. Do you know any poems or songs like this in your language?

Desperate Dan is
A dirty old man.
He washes his face
In a frying-pan.
He brushes his hair
With the leg of a chair –
Desperate Dan is
A dirty old man.

8 That's amazing!

can/can't

1 a Match the titles with the photos.

b 📼 Listen to the radio programme. Which of the five titles is it about?

WALKING ON WATER

BIG BIG BUBBLES

FAST FISH AND DANGEROUS FISH

DIVE WITH YOUR DOG!

THE WALKING DICTIONARY

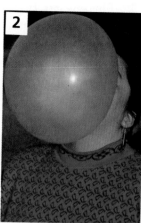

2 a Listen again. Tick (✓) the questions you hear, in the 'Question' boxes.

		Question	Answer
1	Can you speak Chinese?	☐	☐
2	Can you speak Russian?	☐	☐
3	Can you write Russian?	☐	☐
4	Can you speak any African languages?	☐	☐
5	Can you speak any of the languages of West Africa?	☐	☐
6	Can you speak Yoruba?	☐	☐

b What are Mr Ruffle's answers: *Yes, I can* or *No, I can't*? Write ✓ or ✗ in the 'Answer' boxes.

c Listen and check your answers.

d 📼 Listen and repeat the questions and answers.

3 a Look at the photos again. Then read these sentences. Make guesses: true (✓), false (✗) or don't know (**?**).

1 The dog can stay under water for one hour. ☐

2 The dog can stay under water for about five minutes without air. ☐

3 This American girl can only make bubbles with a special sort of bubble-gum. ☐

4 The lizard lives in Costa Rica. It can walk on water … and it can also fly. ☐

5 'The Dictionary Man' can speak and write 58 different languages. ☐

6 The big blue fish can swim very, very fast. It can move at 109 kilometres per hour. ☐

Useful English 📼

✓	**?**	✗
I think that's right. I agree.	Perhaps … It's possible …	No, I don't think so. I'm not sure about that.

b 💬 Work in groups. Discuss the sentences.

4 Read these articles quickly. Check your guesses in Exercise 3.

> **1** Can dogs swim under water? Well, Shadow can. She has her own diving equipment. She can't stay under water for a very long time – only about five minutes, swimming around and watching the fish!

> **2** Susan Williams, from California, can blow very large bubbles. Some of her bubbles are 58 centimetres in diameter! She uses a special sort of bubble-gum.

> **3** The *basilicus basilicus* lizard lives in Costa Rica. It is an amazing lizard. It can walk on water with its long legs and wide feet.

> **4** Mr Ruffle's friends call him 'The Dictionary Man.' He can speak and write 58 different languages! He's a language teacher, of course. He learns new languages when he goes away on holiday.

> **5** One of these fish is very fast and the other is very dangerous. The *cosmopolitan sailfish* can move at 109 kilometres per hour. World champion athletes can only run at 42 kilometres per hour! The *piranha* is very dangerous. Groups of these fish can eat a dead alligator in five minutes.

5 a Who or what can do these things? Match the facts in the two lists.

	A	B
1	run at 42 kilometres per hour	Mr Ruffle
2	eat a dead animal very fast	a lizard in Costa Rica
3	speak a lot of different languages	Susan Williams
4	stay under water for about five minutes	champion athletes
5	make very large bubbles with gum	piranha fish
6	walk across the surface of water	cosmopolitan sailfish
7	move very fast in the water	Shadow, the dog

b Work with a partner. Take turns to check the facts.

A Who or what can run at 42 kilometres per hour?
B World champion athletes.

Learn to learn: using a dictionary (3)

6 a Look at the articles again. Guess the meaning of these words and write your translation.

1 holiday 3 wide 5 diameter
2 equipment 4 athlete

b Check your guesses in a dictionary. Add new words from the articles in Exercise 4 to your vocabulary book.

Work it out: *can*

7 a Look at the five articles again. Underline the sentences with *can* in them. Choose the right answer:

She can swim = 1 She swims
                2 She doesn't swim

b What is the negative form of *can*?

Pronunciation: *can* and *can't*

8 a Listen to *can* in these questions.

b Listen again and repeat.

c Listen to the word *can* in short answers. Is the pronunciation the same as in the questions or different?

d Listen and repeat the questions and answers.

e Listen and answer the questions for yourself.

9 Work with a partner. Ask questions with the phrases in the box. Take turns.

> cook   dance   play football/basketball/volleyball
> play the drums/guitar/piano   ride a bicycle/horse
> speak English   speak another language   swim

A Can you play the guitar?
B No, I can't. Can you ride a bicycle?
A Yes, I can. Can you …?

10 Work in groups. Make a list of six things you can all do. Write sentences about your group.

Do you want to be a champion?

must

1 📼 Listen to a trainer talking to an athlete. Complete the rules.

1 You must organize _____ _____ carefully.

2 You must train _____ _____ .

3 You must _____ _____ _____ the right things.

4 You must _____ _____ _____ _____ before competitions.

5 You must _____ the techniques of _____ _____ .

2 📖 Read and match these titles with the paragraphs of the text. Write the paragraph numbers.

a Where do athletes train? ☐

b Training to be positive ☐

c Who trains, and why? ☐

d Training for good habits ☐

3 Read the article again. Write training rules for an athlete.

Example
Study *You must study the techniques of your sport.*

1 relax
2 sleep
3 win

Work it out: *must*

4 a Look again at the rules in Exercise 3. What does the verb *must* show us? Choose 1, 2 or 3.

1 that something is really amazing to do.
2 that something is very important to do.
3 that something is not very important to do.

b Think of a sport (or hobby or school subject) that you want to be very good at. Write down four things that you must do.

Training to win

1 When you play a game you usually want to play well and win. Some people want to become champions. But becoming a champion takes a lot of time and training.

2 Top athletes usually train in the gym, in a swimming pool or on a running track, but athletes also study in the classroom. 'All of the athletes I work with do a lot of work in the gym or out on the track', says Annie Clark, a trainer at a London athletics club. 'But they must also study all the techniques of their sport, and practise them regularly.'

3 Ms Clark says 'Athletes must learn to relax, eat the right food and drinks and organize their time. They must also get a lot of sleep – that's important.'

4 Learning to win is an important part of their training, too. Athletes must always be positive and want to win.

Days of the week

1 **a** 📼 Look at the programme. Listen to the message and write the changes on the programme.

KING'S SPORTS CENTRE
Evening programme

	7.30	8.00	8.30
Monday	Badminton	Aerobics	Water aerobics
Tuesday	Children's swimming	Football training	Badminton
Wednesday	Badminton	Under 15s' judo	Volleyball training
Thursday	Children's swimming	Aerobics	Basketball training
Friday	Badminton	Volleyball	Water aerobics
Saturday	Under 15s' judo	Football training	Badminton
Sunday	Centre closed		

b 📼 Listen and repeat the days of the week.

2 📼 Listen and complete the message.

Remember

The Games start _____ _____. Meet me _____

_____ o'clock _____ the morning for a run _____

Monday and Wednesday.

You must be at the swimming pool for a swim _____

Tuesday and Thursday _____ eight o'clock.

Work it out: prepositions of time

3 Complete the phrases with *on*, *in* or *at*.

1 _____ six o'clock/night/the weekend

2 _____ the morning/the evening/the summer

3 _____ Monday/Monday morning/Tuesday night

4 💬 Work with a partner. You are both athletes. This is your timetable for next week.

a Write four more things on the timetable (for example, basketball, football training). Don't show your partner.

Monday	Tuesday	Wednesday	Thursday	Friday
6.00 Run	6.00 Swim	6.00 Run	8.00 Swim	8.00 Run
10.00 Video study	10.00	10.00	12.00 Video study	12.00
1.00 L U N C H				
3.00	3.00 Aerobics	3.00	3.00 Gym	3.00
5.00 Aerobics	5.00	5.00 Aerobics	5.00	5.00

b You want to meet, but you are both very busy. Try to find a time. Take turns to ask the questions. Look at the example.

A *Can we meet at twelve o'clock on Thursday?*
B *No, sorry. I must be in class then, for video study.*

Writing: an article

5 You help at a new sports club in your town at the weekend.

a Plan a timetable of five different sports and the times people can come to the club for them.

b ✏️ Write a short article in English for the Visitors' Book to your town and give information about the club. Think of a name and address for the club, too.

Example
The Pacesetter Sports Club is now open. The sports you can play at the club are … You can swim on Monday and Friday at … in the evening.

Where's the money?

1 a Look quickly at the pictures. Don't read the story.
What do you think happens? The club members …

1 get a letter from 'TV 4' with some more money in it.
2 are angry that the others are not there.
3 can't find the money for 'Project OK'.
4 go shopping together.

b Listen and read the story. Check your guess.

1 The next morning

Jane Where are Emma, and the others? I want to go. What time is it, Jack?

Jack It's ten past ten. Let's get a move on!

Dave Sorry I'm late. Carol's at the shops for our Mum.

Jack Er … hang on a minute! We haven't got the money. I … er … oh no! The money – it's in the club.

Jack It's not here!

Jane Oh, Jack! That's not good enough! You're the project boss. What can we do now?

Dave We must find that money or we can't buy anything for the job.

Jack I'm sorry, Jane. I'm really not a very good project boss …

Jane Oh, never mind, Jack. Let's think. What can we do? Any ideas?

Jack Perhaps we can call the police?

Dave No, we don't want to call the police first thing. Where are Emma and Ricky this morning, anyway? Emma always has good ideas.

2 Answer the questions.

   1 Who is late?
   2 Who is not there?
   3 Can they see Emma's note?

Set the pace

3 a Look at the story again. How do you say these things in your language?

   1 Let's get a move on!
   2 Hang on a minute!
   3 That's not good enough!

   b 🔊 Listen and repeat.

   c 🗣 Work in groups. Act out the dialogue.

4 Think of all the things they can't do without the money. One of them is in the story. Compare your ideas with other students.

5 🗣 Work with a partner. Who is your favourite person in the story? Why? Discuss your ideas.

Review

can/can't (cannot)

Remember: She can swim **not** She ~~cans~~ swim.
             You can meet me **not** You can ~~to~~ meet me.

Statements
Positive   *She can speak English.* (Hello, my name's ...)

Negative   *I can't speak Japanese.*

(こんにちは)   (Sorry, I don't understand.)

Questions
Can I help you?   *Can you speak French?*

must

Remember: She must work hard **not** She ~~musts~~ work hard.
             He must come **not** He must ~~to~~ come.

Must is for rules and orders. *You must do your homework.*

Talking about time
Use

in   with parts of the day
      in the morning   in the afternoon   in the evening
      but: *at night*

at   with times (... o'clock)
      at eight o'clock   at quarter past twelve

on   with days of the week
      on Wednesday   on Sunday

1 Write down:

   1 three things you can do.
   2 three things you can't do.
   3 three things you can't understand.
   4 three things you can understand, but think are boring.

2 Imagine that you are an English teacher. Write six rules for the English class.

> *Rules for the English class*
>
> | *Always* | *Never* |
> |---|---|
> | *1 You must always ...* | *1 You must never ...* |
> | *2 You ...* | *2 You ...* |

3 Read these sentences about Britain. Then write similar sentences about your country.

   1 In Britain, people usually start school or work at nine o'clock.
   2 In Britain, people usually have lunch at one o'clock.
   3 In Britain, students usually go home from school at about four o'clock.
   4 In Britain, people usually finish work at five o'clock.
   5 In Britain, people usually have supper at about six or seven o'clock.

Vocabulary

Look at the unit again. Add all the new names of languages, words for sports and hobbies and days of the week to your vocabulary book in word-maps, lists, or family trees. Complete the chart on page 76 of the workbook.

Freewheeling ....

🔊 Listen to the song. Think of a good title for it.

*Can you feel the things I'm feeling
As I sing you this song?
Maybe we can sing together?
Maybe sing the whole night long.*

*Can you listen to the laughter
Going round inside my mind?
Maybe we can laugh together?
Maybe love is there to find.*

*Can you answer all my questions now
And help me make a guess?
Maybe we can dance together?
Maybe no ... BUT MAYBE YES!*

Sing the song.

Travelling

The present continuous

1 a Look at the picture and use your dictionary. Who is on a *package holiday*?

b Tick (✓) the *true* descriptions.

People on package holidays …

1 travel together in large groups. ☐
2 usually stay with local families. ☐
3 usually stay together in one hotel. ☐
4 have a tour guide with them. ☐

c Look at the picture again. Match these names with the other two sorts of tourists in the picture

1 a business traveller
2 an independent traveller

2 📼 Listen to the tour guide and look at the picture again. Who does he see first? … Then? … After that? Write 1, 2 and 3 in the boxes.

the package holiday-makers ☐

the business travellers ☐

the independent travellers ☐

3 Who is doing what? Match the people and the actions.

1 The tour guide is …   looking for the tour guide

2 The police officer is …   answering a question

3 The woman at the bank is not …   talking on the telephone

4 The two independent travellers are …   smiling at the two young visitors

5 The package holiday-makers are …   changing some money

Work it out: the present continuous (1)

4 a Look at the present continuous statements in Exercise 3. Underline the two parts of the verb.

b Complete these rules.

1 Positive: part of the verb _____ (am, is, are) + main verb + - *ing*.

2 Negative: part of the verb _____ (am, is, are) + _____ + main verb + - *ing*.

c Is this statement true or false?

We can use the present continuous to talk about something that is happening at the same time as we speak or write.

d What are the other people in the picture doing?

5 📖 Match these questions with three of the paragraphs below.

Where are the great coral reefs of the world? ☐
What are tourists doing to the world's reefs? ☐
What are coral reefs? ☐

1 Some tourists stay on beautiful islands for their holidays. They bring good business to these places, but sometimes they also bring problems for the environment.

2 Some of the world's great coral reefs are in danger from tourists, for example. Coral reefs take thousands of years to grow from the dead bodies of very small sea animals. They grow from the floor of the sea up to a thousand metres high. They are the home of millions of fish and sea plants.

3 The Australian Great Barrier Reef is one of the world's great reefs. There are other coral reefs along the coasts of Africa, Central America and the Pacific islands.

4 But more and more tourists are visiting the reefs, walking on them and breaking them. People often take pieces of coral home at the end of their holidays. In some countries divers and fishermen are part of the problem, too. They are killing the reefs with pollution from their boats. The great reefs are slowly dying.

6 a Look at the text again. Guess the meaning of these words and write translations.

environment   grow   coast   pollution   boat

b Check your guesses in a dictionary. Add new words from the text to your vocabulary book.

c Read the text again and answer these questions.

1 (paragraph 1) Who or what are *they*? _____
2 (paragraph 2) Who or what are *they*? _____
3 (paragraph 4) Who or what are *them*? _____
4 (paragraph 4) Who or what are *they*? _____

7 a 📼 Listen to the tour guide. Who is mainly causing the problems to the coral reefs?

1 tourists   2 divers   3 fishermen   4 children

b Match the interviewer's questions with the tour guide's answers.

1 Are the tourists causing   Yes, it is.
   these problems?
2 Is the coral dying?   No, it isn't.
3 Are all these divers
   breaking the coral?   Yes, they are.
4 Is the pollution from their
   boats killing the coral?   No, they aren't.

Work it out: the present continuous (2)

8 a Look at the questions and short answers in Exercise 7. Complete the chart.

be	Main verb + - *ing*
I _____ / _____ not	
She _____ /isn't	causing the problem.
They _____ /aren't	

Statement:	He _____ causing the problem.
Question:	_____ he causing the problem?
Short answer:	Yes, he _____ .

b Change the questions in Exercise 7 into statements.

Example
Are the tourists causing the problems?

The tourists are causing the problems.

Having a wonderful time …?

Adverbs and adjectives

1 Look at the pictures on the postcards. What sort of holiday are these people having? Write the letters next to the pictures.

A   a skiing holiday
B   a camping holiday
C   a cruise
D   a city holiday
E   a tropical beach holiday
F   a walking holiday

2 a 📖 Read the postcards. Only one writer really is having a wonderful time – which one? Write 1, 2 or 3. _____

1

POST CARD

Dear Mum and Dad,
This is not my dream holiday. The weather's awful: I'm sitting in our hotel room and it's raining quite hard outside. All the other people in our group are playing cards or sitting miserably under the umbrellas near the pool. In fact, everything's quite miserable here – I can't wait to get home.

Love, P.

Mr and Mrs Davies
41 Hart Road
Oxford
OX5 ISS

2

POST CARD

Hi! This is great. We're having a really good time. We're staying in a comfortable small hotel in the mountains. Right now the sun is shining warmly – it's about 23° today. I have skiing lessons every morning and then I practise on the slopes every afternoon. I'm getting quite good. See you soon!

Sam xx

Anna Richards
28 Homefield Avenue
London SW28 4RT
England

3

POST CARD

Dear Mum,
Summer camp is going badly. I'm writing this in my tent and it's raining steadily again out there. Water is coming through the tent. Everything's wet. The food is terrible. I'm hungry all the time – and I don't like any of the other children here. Please send me some money immediately. I want to come home. Love, Terry.

Mrs Rachel Duffy
158 Museum Street
Edinburgh
Scotland

b Match the texts and the pictures of the three postcards.

Text 1 = picture _____

Text 2 = picture _____

Text 3 = picture _____

3 🗩 Work in a group. Which sort of holiday in Exercise 1 is your group's 'dream holiday'? Why?

Work it out: adverbs of manner

4 **a** We make regular adverbs of manner with an adjective + *-ly*. Look back at the texts. Find the adverbs of manner and complete these lists.

	Adjectives	Adverbs of manner
1	warm	_____
2	bad	_____
3	_____	miserably
4	immediate	_____

b There is a spelling change for adjectives ending in *-y*: take away the *-y* and add *-ily*. Write the adverb.

Example
hungry → hungrily

5 steady _____

c *Good* has an irregular adverb: *good → well*. *Hard* and *fast* are also irregular. Check them in your dictionary. Add all the new adverbs to your vocabulary book.

d Use these verbs and adverbs to make six true sentences about yourself.

Example
I can't run fast.

Verbs	Adverbs
cook run sing	fast hard
speak English swim work	slowly well

5 Work with a partner. Ask *What can you do?*

The weather

1 **a** Listen to this phone call. One of the postcard writers is speaking. Who – 1, 2 or 3?

b Listen again. Choose two adverbs from the box and complete the sentence.

This person is speaking _____ and _____ .

> carefully   loudly   miserably   nicely   quietly
> warmly

Vocabulary: the weather

What's the **wea**ther like?
It's **terr**ible!
It's **beau**tiful!
It's **hot**.
It's **warm**.
It's **cold**.

The **sun**'s **shi**ning.
It's **rai**ning.
It's **sno**wing.
It's **su**nny.
It's **clou**dy.
It's **win**dy.

2 Listen and tick (✓) the phrases that you hear.

Pronunciation: /ŋ/

3 **a** Listen and repeat the phrases.

b Listen and look at this weather map. Answer the questions on the cassette.

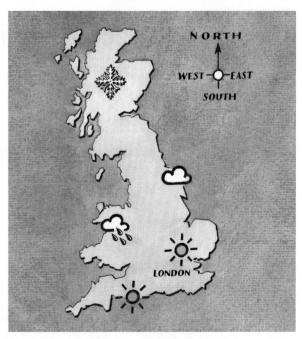

c What's the weather like today in your area? Write two or three sentences about it.

Writing: a postcard

4 You are on holiday with your family in one part of your country or in one of the main cities. Look at the three postcards again. Write a postcard to a friend at home.

What is the weather like? What are you doing? What are the other members of your family doing? Are you 'having a wonderful time'?

Detective work

1 a Look at the pictures. Are these statements true or false?

Picture 3: Jack is talking to Ricky. ☐

Picture 3: Ricky and Carol are laughing. ☐

Picture 3: Ricky is sitting with Carol. ☐

Picture 4: Jack is laughing too. ☐

b 📼 Listen and read. Check your answers.

Jack Let's phone Emma's place and talk to her. Maybe she can think of something. Have you got 10p for the phone?
Jane Yes, sure.

At the phone box

Ricky Hi, Jack … Emma? Yes, she's here now. Carol's here too.

Jack Emma isn't at home. Maybe she's doing some shopping.
Jane Try Ricky's place. She's often there.

Emma The money? Yes, of course I've got it! Haven't you got my message? It's on the Coffee Corner.
Jack You've got the money? Oh, great! A message? No … What's going on over there? Why are Ricky and Carol laughing? Come on, Emma! You can tell me!
Emma I can't explain now, Jack. See you in half an hour.

Jane What's going on, Jack?
Jack Well, she's got the money. That's the main thing. But they're laughing at us! I don't like it …

2 🗣 Work with a partner. Ask and answer about these pictures.

Example
Picture 3/Jack
A *What's Jack doing in Picture 3?*
B *He's talking to Ricky on the phone.*

1 Picture 1/Jane   3 Picture 3/Carol
2 Picture 3/Emma   4 Picture 4/Jack

3 **a** Look at the story again. How do you say these things in your language?

  1 Yes, sure.   3 What's going on?
  2 Ricky's place.

b Listen and repeat.

4 🖊 In picture 2 we do not see or hear the complete conversation between Ricky and Jack. Write the complete conversation.

5 🗪 Work with a partner. Act out the phone call. Practise the complete phone conversation.

6 What are Emma, Carol and Ricky laughing about? What are they planning to do?

Review

The present continuous

Positive statements	am/is/are + main verb + *-ing* *It's raining.*
Negative statements	am/is/are + not (n't) + main verb + *-ing* *It isn't raining now.*
Questions (Yes/No) and short answers	*Is it raining? Yes, it is./No, it isn't.*

We often use the present continuous to talk about what is happening at or near the time we are speaking or writing.

Adverbs of manner

Adjective			Adverb
loud			loudly
slow	+ *-ly*	→	slowly
noisy	+ *-ily*	→	noisily
			Irregular adverbs
good	→		well
fast	→		fast
hard	→		hard

We use adverbs of manner to describe the way that something happens.

They're walking quickly.

---

1 **a** Look at these puzzle pictures and answer these two questions. What is it? What is it doing?

It's a cat. It's climbing up a tree.

  1 (play)   2 (stand)   3 (ride)   4 (climb)

b 🗪 Work with a partner. Check your guesses together. Do you agree? Ask and answer.

2 **a** Find six adjectives in the word square. Write the adverbs from the adjectives.

A	D	M	B	H
S	N	P	A	U
L	O	U	D	N
O	I	J	V	G
W	S	Z	D	R
F	Y	W	L	Y
G	O	O	D	A

Example

loud → loudly

b Write sentences with the adverbs in them.

Vocabulary

Look at the unit again. Add all the new words for the weather, directions, and holidays to your vocabulary book.

Freewheeling ....

a Look at the weather symbols. Complete the chant.

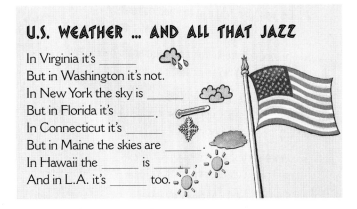

b Listen and check your answers.

c Listen again and say the chant.

Diet and lifestyle

The present simple and continuous

3 📼 Listen to Sally. Complete the questionnaire for her and work out her score.

4 Is Sally telling the truth? Look at the pictures. This is what she is doing today. Describe her day.
Sally's going to school by car.

1 a Look at the picture. Use your dictionary to find any new words for food and drink.

b 💬 Work with a partner. Divide the words into these two groups: healthy food and junk food.

2 Look at the diet and lifestyle questionnaire. Answer the questions for yourself. Then ask a partner. Find out your scores on page 110.

Are you a couch potato?

Answer these questions and find out!

1 Do you eat sweets and chocolate every day?
a) Yes, I love them!   **b)** Not every day.   **c)** No.

2 Do you take sugar in tea and coffee?
a) Yes.   **b)** No.

3 Do you eat fresh fruit and vegetables every day?
a) Yes.   **b)** No.

4 How do you get to school?
a) I walk.   **b)** I ride my bicycle.   **c)** I come by bus.
d) I come by car.

5 What sort of exercise do you take?
a) I play sports.   **b)** I walk to the shops.   **c)** I don't.

6 Do you watch TV every evening?
a) Yes, two or three hours.   **b)** Yes, for about an hour.
c) No, not every evening.

Work it out:
the present simple and continuous

5 a Look at what Sally says about her lifestyle.
I don't eat sweets or chocolate.
But today she's eating chocolate.

Write the correct tense.
To talk about regular, everyday actions:

_____

To talk about actions happening 'at the moment':

_____

b 💬 Work with a partner. Discuss what Sally says about her lifestyle and what she is doing in the pictures.

A Sally says she doesn't eat chocolate.
B But in the pictures she's eating some chocolate.

Numbers over 100

1 Look at this headline from a newspaper article.

British children are getting **fat!**

a 👓 Work in groups. Why are British children getting fat? Guess.

b Read the article and check your guess.

> Yes, it's true! British children are getting fat, but they are also growing in other ways, too. Studies show that the height and weight of modern ten-year-olds are different from the height and weight of their parents at ten. British ten-year-olds are now on average 141 centimetres tall (138–139 cm in 1972). The same studies show a 17% increase in weight.
>
> The studies don't give reasons for this, but we can guess that the children are changing for two main reasons: diet and exercise. These days children eat healthy food a lot of the time, and this explains the increase in height to 141 cm, but they also eat a lot of junk food, for example, sweets, chips, cakes and biscuits. After school, many of today's children sit down all evening. They watch TV, listen to music, or do their homework, but they often don't take any exercise.

2 Match these words with the examples.

1	weight	160 cm
2	height	swimming, walking, aerobics
3	diet	75 kilos
4	exercise	meat, bread, fruit

3 Are these sentences true or false? Write ✓ or ✗.

1 Today's ten-year-olds are the same height as their parents at ten.
2 On average, ten-year-old children in Scotland and England are about 139 cm tall.
3 Some modern children have a bad diet.
4 These days a lot of children don't take any exercise.

Work it out: numbers over 100

4 a Look at these large numbers.

1,000   a thousand
10,000   ten thousand
1,000,000   a million

b Write the numbers.
Examples
a hundred and thirty-eight *138*
one thousand, two hundred   *1,200*

1 two thousand, seven hundred and thirty-six
2 thirty thousand, two hundred and five
3 three hundred and twenty-eight thousand, five hundred and fourteen
4 five million, two hundred thousand, four hundred and ten

c 📼 Listen. Say the numbers after the cassette.

d Write these numbers in full.

275 *two hundred and seventy-five*
502 *five hundred and two*

1 199   2 415   3 707   4 6,832   5 958,014
6 3,186,924

5 a 👓 Work in groups. Ask: *What is your height?* Work out the average for your group.

b What is the height or length of these things? Match the places with the numbers in the box.

1	Mount Everest	4	the CN Tower
2	the Statue of Liberty	5	the Nile
3	the Great Barrier Reef		

46 metres   553 metres   8,848 metres
2,010 kilometres   6,695 kilometres

Example
I think the height of Mount Everest is …

c 📼 Listen and check your answers.

Pocket money

How much/many?

Vocabulary: buying and spending

1 Look at the pictures. Match each picture with a label from the box.

> books and magazines   clothes   computers
> food and drink   going out   music
> special occasions   sports

2 🔊 Listen. Martin, Laura and Gemma are friends. They are talking about their pocket money. What does 'pocket money' mean?

3 🔊 Listen to some more of their conversation. Look at the pie charts and write the correct name next to each chart.

1 _____   2 _____

Work it out: *How much ...? How many ...?*

4 a   Complete these questions with *much* or *many*.

1   How _____ pocket money do you get?

2   How _____ magazines do you buy a month?

3   How _____ computer games do you buy?

4   How _____ money do your parents give you?

b   🔊 Listen and repeat the questions.

c   Write *How much ...?* or *How many ...?* under the pictures.

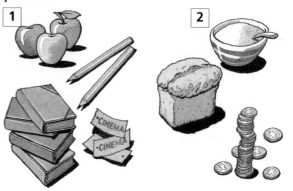

_____   _____

Useful English 🔊

> I get about thirty pounds a month.
> I spend about ten pounds on cassettes/books/clothes.
> Lucky you!
> 50% = half   25% = a quarter
> 33% = a third   66% = two-thirds

5 Look at the pictures in Exercise 1 again.

a   Write a list of five things you spend money on.

b   💬 Work with a partner. Ask and answer.

A   What do you spend your money on?
B   I buy cassettes, magazines and clothes.
A   How many cassettes do you buy a month?
B   I buy about ...
A   How much money do you spend on cassettes a month?
B   Oh, I spend about .../I spend a quarter/half of my money on cassettes.

Writing: describing your spending

6 ✎ Write to a magazine about your spending habits.

a Plan your writing. Draw a pie chart to work out your spending habits for one month.

b How do you want to describe your spending?

£10.50/fifty per cent/a half

c Write a paragraph for the magazine. Write about 50–60 words.

Months and dates

1 📼 Look at the calendar. Listen and repeat the names of the months.

2 a Find your birthday and two other important dates and circle them.

	M T W T F S S M T W T F S S M T W T F S S M T W T F S S M T W T F S S M T
JANUARY	1 2 3 4 5 6 7 8 9 10 11 12 13 14 15 16 17 18 19 20 21 22 23 24 25 26 27 28 29 30 31
FEBRUARY	1 2 3 4 5 6 7 8 9 10 11 12 13 14 15 16 17 18 19 20 21 22 23 24 25 26 27 28 29
MARCH	1 2 3 4 5 6 7 8 9 10 11 12 13 14 15 16 17 18 19 20 21 22 23 24 25 26 27 28 29 30 31
APRIL	1 2 3 4 5 6 7 8 9 10 11 12 13 14 15 16 17 18 19 20 21 22 23 24 25 26 27 28 29 30
MAY	1 2 3 4 5 6 7 8 9 10 11 12 13 14 15 16 17 18 19 20 21 22 23 24 25 26 27 28 29 30 31
JUNE	1 2 3 4 5 6 7 8 9 10 11 12 13 14 15 16 17 18 19 20 21 22 23 24 25 26 27 28 29 30
JULY	1 2 3 4 5 6 7 8 9 10 11 12 13 14 15 16 17 18 19 20 21 22 23 24 25 26 27 28 29 30 31
AUGUST	1 2 3 4 5 6 7 8 9 10 11 12 13 14 15 16 17 18 19 20 21 22 23 24 25 26 27 28 29 30 31
SEPTEMBER	1 2 3 4 5 6 7 8 9 10 11 12 13 14 15 16 17 18 19 20 21 22 23 24 25 26 27 28 29 30
OCTOBER	1 2 3 4 5 6 7 8 9 10 11 12 13 14 15 16 17 18 19 20 21 22 23 24 25 26 27 28 29 30 31
NOVEMBER	1 2 3 4 5 6 7 8 9 10 11 12 13 14 15 16 17 18 19 20 21 22 23 24 25 26 27 28 29 30
DECEMBER	1 2 3 4 5 6 7 8 9 10 11 12 13 14 15 16 17 18 19 20 21 22 23 24 25 26 27 28 29 30 31

b 📼 Listen and circle the OK Club members' birthdays on the calendar.

Pronunciation: ordinal numbers

3 a Listen again and repeat the dates.

b 📼 Listen and say these numbers.

fourth fifth sixth seventh eighth ninth
tenth eleventh twelfth thirteenth

Work it out: ordinal numbers

4 a Read these numbers and words.

1st = first	2nd = second	3rd = third
15th = fifteenth	20th = twentieth	
22nd = twenty-second	29th = twenty-ninth	

b Write these numbers in words. Use the words above and in Exercise 3 to help you.

2nd 13th 18th 21st 24th 30th

5 📼 Listen and repeat these dates.

What's the date today?	
We say	**We write**
(It's) the first of October.	1st October
(It's) the twelfth of May.	12th May
(It's) the twentieth of June.	20th June

6 ✎ Work in groups of four. Find out and write your group's birthdays.

A When's your birthday? B It's on …

7 Tell other students the date of your birthday. Can you find another student with the same birthday?

Buying a present

1 📼 Laura is buying a birthday present.

a Listen. What kind of shop is she in? Who is the present for?

b Listen again. Write the shop assistant's questions.

c Listen again. There are three prices in the dialogue. Tick (✓) the right way of saying them.

1 £22.50 a twenty-two and a half pounds
         b twenty-two fifty
2 £20.00 a twenty pounds
         b twenty pounds and no pence
3 £18.99 a eighteen point nine nine pounds
         b eighteen ninety-nine

2 💬 Work with a partner. Make a new dialogue.

A You are the shop assistant. Use the questions from the dialogue. The shirts are £15.99 or £21.50.

B You are the customer. You want to buy a shirt for your brother. Think of the colour. You have £17.

Start the dialogue:

A Good morning. Can I help you?

B Yes, I'm looking for a birthday present.

The trick

1 a Before you read, look quickly at the pictures. Answer the questions.

1 Where are they in Picture 3?
2 What is Emma giving to Jack in Picture 4?
3 What is she giving to Jane and Dave in Picture 5?

b Which of these words do you think you will find in the story? Tick them (✓). Use a dictionary if necessary.

> chips cinema exercise explain plan shy tickets

2 📼 Listen and read. Check your answers.

Emma OK, so Dave is shy and he can't ask Jane to go to the cinema with him …
Carol Right, but he really likes her.
Emma And Jane's shy too. So we help them a bit, OK? We buy two cinema tickets for tomorrow evening, but we tell them that we've all got tickets. So they go to the cinema together, without us!
Ricky That's brilliant, Emma!

Ricky What about Jack? Do we tell him?
Carol No, I don't think that's a good idea – you know he likes Jane too.

Cashier So, two tickets for 6.20 on Friday 7th.
Emma Now let's go to the club.

Emma Here's the money, Jack. Next time, don't leave it in the Coffee Corner!
Jack Oh, thanks, Emma. I must just check it and finish that list of things for 'Project OK'. See you in a minute.

Emma And here are the cinema tickets. Let's all meet at the cinema at six o'clock. OK?
Jane Thanks, Emma. Six is fine.
Dave What's the film, Carol?
Carol Er …

Set the pace

3 **a** How do you say these phrases in your language?

    1 That's brilliant!   3 See you in a minute.
    2 What about Jack?   4 Six is fine.

  b 📼 Listen and repeat.

4 This is Emma's plan but the parts of the plan are in the wrong order. Write numbers in the boxes to show the right order.

  a Dave and Jane arrive at the cinema. They wait outside but the others do not come. ☐

  b She tells them that all the others have tickets for the film, too, but this is not true. ☐

  c Emma buys two tickets for a film at the local cinema. ☐

  d Jane and Dave go into the cinema together and see the film without the others. ☐

  e She gives the tickets to Jane and Dave. ☐

5 🗣 Work with a partner. What do you think of Emma's plan? Is it clever or is it silly? Discuss it.

Review

The present simple and the present continuous

Present simple
Facts: *My brother lives in New York.*
Regular actions: *Mum starts work at 7.00 a.m.*

Present continuous
Actions at or near the time we are speaking or writing:

What's Dad doing? He's cooking lunch.
I'm learning English this year.

How much ...? and *How many ...?*

We use *How much ...?* with uncountable nouns.
How much milk/time/money/water have you got?

We use *How many ...?* with countable nouns.
How many apples/pens/T-shirts/cassettes have you got?

Ordinal numbers

Ordinal numbers end in *-st, -nd, -rd* or *-th*.

1st = first, 2nd = second, 3rd = third, 4th = fourth,
25th = twenty-fifth, 46th = forty-sixth,
79th = seventy-ninth

1 🗣 Work with a partner. Find a picture from the OK Club story and ask questions.

Example

A *Look at picture 1 on page 46. Who's the woman?*
B *She's a TV producer.*
A *What does she usually do?*
B *She makes TV programmes.*
A *What's she doing in the picture?*
B *She's talking to the teenagers about the club.*

2 **a** Write five questions for your partner with *How much ...?* or *How many ...?*

  Examples
  How many books are there in your school bag?
  How much money have you got with you today?

  b 🗣 Ask your partner the questions. Take turns.

3 Think of five important dates for you and write them.

Example
18/6 the eighteenth of June. It's my birthday.

Vocabulary

Look at the unit again. Add all the new verbs for everyday actions, food words, per cent and fractions, months and dates to your vocabulary book.

Freewheeling ....

🗣 Play a game. Work with two more students. Mime an action in a 'manner' (for example, slowly, noisily). Your partners guess your action and manner. Take turns.

Here are some ideas to help you:

Verbs: *sit down, walk, run, write, sing, play, eat*
Adverbs: *quickly, carefully, quietly, easily, noisily, hungrily*

Consolidation

Grammar

1 Describe what Kevin is doing in each picture.

In picture A Kevin's going to school.

2 Complete this text about the pictures.

It's Monday. Kevin usually has school on Monday; he ¹ _goes_ to school at eight o'clock in the morning. But this Monday he's on holiday. It's eight o'clock in the morning and Kevin ²(not) _____: he's in bed. He ³ _____ a magazine. Of course, when it's school time, Kevin ⁴(not) _____ magazines in bed in the morning.

It's Tuesday. Kevin usually ⁵ _____ to school on Tuesday, and in the afternoon he ⁶ _____ the piano in his music lesson. This Tuesday afternoon he ⁷(not) _____ the piano because he's on holiday, and he ⁸ _____ football in the park with some friends.

3 Write about the other days in the pictures.

Example
Wednesday/often/after school
It's Wednesday. On Wednesday Kevin often plays chess after school, but this Wednesday he isn't playing chess. He's playing computer games …

1 Thursday/sometimes/after school
2 Friday/usually/after supper

4 Work in groups. Find students who can do unusual things!

a Write two more questions, then ask and answer all the questions.

Can you …

1 say this tongue-twister?
  The sun's shining on shy Susan's sleeping sister.
2 dance to fast disco music?
3 write your name backwards?

  ᴙoυɾ υɐɯǝ

4 play an unusual musical instrument? (What?)
5 cook an interesting meal? (What?)
6 play a sport very well? (What?)

b Write about your group.

In our group Michael can play basketball very well. Bridget can make a pizza, but she can't make an omelette!

Coffeepotting

- I've got an idea.
- Can you coffeepot in the park?
- Do you usually coffeepot carefully?
- Are you coffeepotting now?

5 🔊 Listen to the game. Then play it in groups. Take turns to think of an action. You can ask only ten questions to find the action, then use the verb in a sentence.

Vocabulary

1 Circle the odd one out in each group.

1 north   east   (rain)   south
2 tennis   shopping   football   volleyball
3 rain   sun   snow   gym
4 weight   height   tall   length
5 beach   city   sea   mountain
6 Monday   Thursday   Saturday   March
7 old   round   square   triangular
8 sweets   chocolate   chips   cake

2 Find the opposites of these words in the box.

different   evening   hot   impossible   loud
never   receive   slowly   true   unhealthy   well

1 always _____   7 cold _____
2 false _____   8 quiet _____
3 morning _____   9 possible _____
4 same _____   10 fast _____
5 send _____   11 healthy _____
6 badly _____

3 a Complete these words with *a, e, i, o* or *u*. Then write them in the correct lists. (There are three for each list.)

_ _ r _ b _ cs   _ nv _ nt _ r
_ _ rp _ rt   l _ br _ ry
b _ _ ch   m _ _ nt _ _ n
c _ k _   sh _ p _ ss _ st _ nt
ch _ ss   sp _ rts c _ ntr _
ch _ ps   sw _ _ ts
c _ r _ l r _ _ f   v _ ll _ yb _ ll
d _ v _ r

Jobs: *inventor,* _____

Places in (or near) a town: _____

Sports and games: _____

Places outside a town: _____

Food and drink: _____

b Add two more words to each list.

Communication

1 a Complete this dialogue with your own words.

In a shop
A Good _morning_. How can I _____ _____ ?
B I'm looking for a **birthday** present.
A Who _____ _____ _____ ?
B It's for my **brother**.
A What sort of present are you _____ _____ ?
B I'm not sure, maybe a CD.
A What kind of _____ does he like?
B He _____ **pop music**.
A Well, this is a new CD with all the _____ from **last year**.
B Oh, that's a good idea. _____ _____ is it?
A It's £24. It's **a double CD**.
B Oh dear, I've only got **£15**.
A Ah, well, here's _____ _____ , by *Blue Aquarium*. This is only _____ **pounds**.
B That's good. Yes, I'd like that.
A Here you are.
B Thanks.

b 🔊 Listen. Are your answers the same as the words on the cassette?

2 🗨 Work with a partner. Make a new dialogue. Change the words in **bold**. Then act out your dialogue to another pair.

Project: a sports survey

1 a 🔊 Listen to the sounds of some sports. Match the sounds with eight of the pictures. Write the correct letters.

Example

l = J

b Now match all the sports with their names.

aerobics _F_   horse-riding ___

badminton ___   judo ___

basketball ___   riding a bike ___

billiards ___   running ___

cricket ___   swimming ___

diving ___   tennis ___

football ___   volleyball ___

c Add any new sports or activities to your vocabulary book.

Reading

2 📖 Read the text about sports in a British school and answer the questions.

1 Which sport or activity must all the students do?
2 Which sports do boys do in the winter?
3 Which sports do girls do in the summer?

In our school we can do a lot of sports. The school says we must all learn to swim, so we go swimming once a week all the year. We can choose to do other sports, too. The girls and boys sometimes play different sports. For example, about 90% of the boys but only half of the girls go running.

BOYS

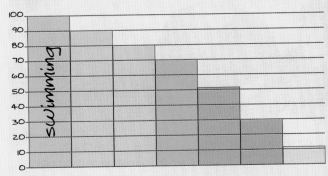

In winter we do some sports and in summer we do other sports. In winter about 80% of the boys play football. Just over half of the boys play basketball, but only a few play volleyball (they think it's a girls' game). In summer about 70% of the boys play cricket and only 30% play tennis.

GIRLS

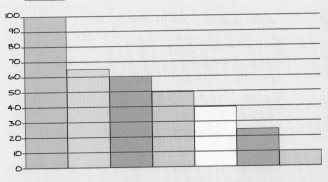

In winter, the girls can now play football, too, but only a few choose it. About two-thirds of the girls play volleyball, and a quarter play basketball. In summer a lot of the girls play tennis, about 60%, and about 40% do aerobics.

3 Read the text again, carefully, and write the sports on the bar charts.

Listening

4 🔲 Listen to four British teenagers and complete the chart with the sports they play.

1   Michael   *football, billiards*

2   Kelly   _____

3   James   _____

4   Fiona   _____

5 Complete this chart. Use the text and listen to the cassette again to help you.

do	go	play	ride
aerobics	running	badminton	a horse

Speaking

6 🗣️ Work with a partner. Discuss the sports in Exercise 1.

A   Can you swim/play ...?

B   Yes, I can.

B   No, I can't.

A   Do you often ...?

A   Oh. Can you ...?

B   Yes, I can.

B   Yes, I do.   B   No, I don't.

A   Do you often ...?

A   When do you ...?   A   OK. Can you play ...

7 a   Work in groups. Look at the questionnaire and complete the questions.

Sports survey

	Name	Name	Name	Name
1 Which sports do you play?				
2 How many times a week do you ____?				
3 Where _____?				

b   🗣️ Ask questions to complete the questionnaire.

Before you write

8 Make a bar chart for your group.

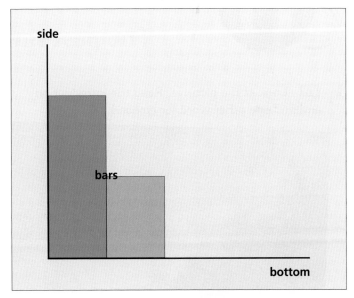

a   Count the sports in your questionnaire and write their names on the bottom of the chart.

b   Write the percentages on the side of the chart.

c   How many students do each sport?

In a group of four: 4 = 100%, 3 = 75%, 2 = 50%, 1 = 25%

d   Draw the bars for each sport on the chart.

Writing

9 Look at the information in your bar chart and in your questionnaire.

a   ✏️ Write about the survey. Use the text and Exercise 5 to help you.

In our group, we play/do ...
All of us .../Half of us ...
... per cent of us ...

b   Put your bar chart and your paragraph together on a piece of paper. Display it for the class.

Check your vocabulary book

Before you start Unit 11 check that all the new words in Units 6-10 are in your vocabulary book.

Typhoon Opal

The past simple: *be*

1 📖 Look at the pictures. Read the introduction and find one other word for *typhoon*.

In June 1997 I was on holiday with my family on an island in the Pacific. We were in a small house near the beach. One day there was a violent storm. The wind was at 230 kilometres an hour and there was very heavy rain. The people of those islands call these storms 'typhoons'. This is my own experience of Typhoon Opal.

2 📖 Read the sentences about Typhoon Opal. Does each sentence take place before the typhoon, during the typhoon or after the typhoon?

1 The wind was extremely strong. It wasn't possible to stand up in it.
2 It was a beautiful sunny day. The sky was clear and blue.
3 In the 'eye' (the middle) of the typhoon there were about twenty minutes with no wind or rain. It was strangely quiet.
4 Our house wasn't badly damaged, but some houses were in pieces.
5 There weren't any undamaged buildings in the whole place.
6 There wasn't any wind that morning. It was very quiet and still.

3 📼 Listen and check your answers.

4 a Listen again and look at the photos. Guess the meaning of these words.

　1 extremely　2 damaged　3 still

　b Check your guesses in a dictionary.

5 a 📼 Listen to part of a phone call from London after the typhoon. Order these parts of the conversation. Write 1 to 6.

Yes, there was quite a lot of damage. ☐

Yes, we were. Right in the middle! ☐

Yes, we are. We're all safe and well. ☐ *1*

Yes, we were. We were in a little house. ☐

Interesting? No, it wasn't. It was terrifying. ☐

No, they weren't. They were all damaged. ☐

　b Listen again. This time, answer the questions.

Work it out: the past simple (1)

6 **a** Underline the past simple verbs (*was*, *were*) in Exercises 1 and 2. Then complete the chart.

	Positive	Negative
I	_____	wasn't
you	were	weren't
he/she/it	_____	_____
we/they	_____	_____

b It is now July. Which months can we use *was* or *were* with? Tick them (✓).

April ☐   June ☐   August ☐
October ☐   December ☐

c Write *Past simple* on the correct line.

```
                    now
        ┌────────────┼────────────┐
      June         July        August
```
_____   _____   _____

7 **a** Complete these statements from the cassette with *was*, *wasn't*, *were* or *weren't*.

1 We _____ ready for a terrifying experience like that.

2 It _____ about eleven o'clock.

3 Our house _____ too badly damaged.

4 We _____ down at the beach one morning.

b Match the three questions and answers.

What sort of experience
was it?   Yes, it was.

Was it a really awful
experience?   No, they weren't.

Were any of the houses   It was terrifying!
undamaged?

Pronunciation: *was* and *were*

8 **a** 📼 Listen to these sentences with *was* and *were*. Which one in each group is different?

1 It was a lovely day.
  Was she in the house?   Yes, she was.
2 We were very frightened.
  Were they with the children?   Yes, they were.

b Listen again and repeat all the sentences.

9 🗣 Work with a partner. Ask and answer questions about yesterday.

Example
A *Where were you yesterday at seven o'clock?*
B *I was …*
A *Who were you with?*

10 Which of these things do you think were true for the English writer and his family after Typhoon Opal? Tick the boxes (✓).

1 They were all very tired.   ☐
2 They were very thirsty.   ☐
3 All their clothes were wet.   ☐
4 They were quite hungry.   ☐
5 They were very hot.   ☐
6 They were extremely frightened.   ☐
7 They were happy.   ☐

Useful English 📼

I think it was awful.	Why?
Because (there was a lot of noise.)	
I don't think it was bad.	Why not?
Because (they were OK.)	

11 🗣 Work with a partner. What do you think about the statements in Exercise 10? Give your reasons. Take turns.

A I think they were all very tired.
B Why?
A Because …

12 ✏ Write about your own experiences. Write about times when you were:

1 extremely hot   3 very happy   5 extremely tired
2 very frightened 4 very wet   6 completely lost

Answer these questions about each experience.

When was this experience? Where were you? Who were you with?

Survival

The past simple: *have, go*

1 Look at the diagram and the photo. What do you think this story is about? Guess.

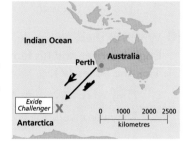

a A training exercise for the crew of an Australian Navy ship

b A yacht race round the coast of Australia

c An amazing rescue of a yachtsman from the ocean

2 📖 Read the story. Check your guess. Underline the words which help you.

3 Read the story again. Are these statements true or false? Write ✓ or ✗.

1 The yachts had very bad weather for the race. ☐

2 Bullimore didn't have any warning before his boat went over, upside-down. ☐

3 The yacht didn't go down immediately. ☐

4 Bullimore didn't have any food. ☐

5 An Australian ship went to help him. ☐

6 Some men from the Australian plane went over to Bullimore's yacht in a small boat. ☐

A race to rescue

On Sunday 5th January 1997, Tony Bullimore was in his yacht, the *Exide Challenger*. He was 2,240 kilometres south west of Australia in the Indian Ocean.

He was in a yacht race, but there was an awful storm. There were strong winds and his yacht went up and down violently on the huge waves.

Suddenly – BANG! – there was one enormous wave and the yacht went over, upside-down. Bullimore had freezing water all round him but there was a small space above the freezing water and the yacht didn't go down. He was extremely cold. He had a little fresh water and some chocolate, but he didn't have any other food.

He also had a radio with an emergency signal and an Australian Navy ship went to rescue him. But there wasn't much time and it was a long way from Australia.

Four days later, on Thursday 9th, an Australian plane went over the yacht, and the ship was only five hours behind it. At midday the ship was next to the yacht. Some men went over to the yacht in a small boat and Bullimore was there – alive and safe! It was an amazing rescue.

Work it out: the past simple (2)

4 a Complete these sentences with *had* and *went*.

Example
I went to Antarctica. I had a difficult journey.

1 Tony Bullimore _____ an amazing experience.
   He _____ to the Indian Ocean in his yacht.

2 The Australian ship and plane _____ to rescue
   Bullimore. They _____ a long way to go.

What is the negative of these verbs in the past simple?

b Complete the verbs in the next part of Bullimore's story.

1 Tony Bullimore _____ _____ back to England immediately.

2 He _____ into hospital in Perth for three or four days.

3 His wife, Lalel, _____ to Australia to be with him.

4 Bullimore _____ _____ any idea that he was famous!

Past simple questions

1 a 📼 Listen to an Australian TV interview with one of the rescuers. Which of the questions do you hear?

> 1 Did you go across to Bullimore's yacht in the rescue boat?
>
> 2 Did you have any real hope that he was alive in there?
>
> 3 Did you have diving equipment in the rescue boat?
>
> 4 Did you have a doctor with you in the rescue boat?
>
> 5 Did you go into the water to help him?
>
> 6 How many men went with you in the rescue boat?
>
> 7 What were Bullimore's first words to you?

b Listen to the interview again. What were the rescuer's answers to the questions?
Yes, I did/No, I didn't.
or *Yes, we did/No, we didn't.*

c 🗣 Work with a partner.

A You are the interviewer. Ask the questions.
B You are the rescuer. Answer the interviewer's questions.

Work it out: the past simple (3)

2 a Look at Exercise 1. Complete these questions and answers.

1 '_____ Tony Bullimore have any food with him?'
   'Yes, he _____.'

2 '_____ he go home to England immediately after the rescue?'
   'No, he _____.'

3 'Where _____ he _____ after the rescue?'
   'He _____ to Perth.'

b Complete the past simple chart.

Questions	Short answers
Did you _____ it?	Yes, I did.
Did he have it?	No, he didn't.
Did she have it?	Yes, she _____.
Did _____ have it?	No, they _____.

3 🗣 Work with a partner. Ask and answer about one of your bad experiences from page 77.

Where were you?
Who were you with?
What clothes did you have on?
What did you have with you (food/water)?
What things didn't you have?
Where did you go? Why?

Writing: a short story

4 a Plan a story with the questions from Exercise 3.

b ✏️ Write the story. Use *had/didn't have* and *went/didn't go*.

c Check the past simple verbs in your story.

Ricky the spy

1 What can you remember from the Unit 10 story?

 1 Who had a plan? _____

 2 Did Emma buy two tickets? _____

 3 Who went to the cinema? _____

2 **a** Look at the pictures and guess. about this part of the story.

 1 Where are they in picture 1?

 2 What is Ricky telling the others about?

 3 In Picture 4, why are they laughing?

 b 📼 Listen and read. Check your guesses.

Two days later

Ricky Right, then. Before Jack and Dave come back, do you want to hear the story of Jane and Dave at the cinema?

Emma Yes, go on, Ricky. Tell us.

Ricky Dave and Jane went to the cinema yesterday evening. The film was at 6.20. Jane was there at 5.50 … and Dave was there at 6.00. They both had their tickets.

Ricky I was across the street. They didn't see me.

Ricky Jane and Dave went into the cinema. It was *brilliant*! Dave's face was really red. I had a really good time.

Jane So *that* was the mystery of the meeting at your place the other morning!

Ricky That's right! It was Emma's idea really.

Emma Yes, but *you* were the spy, Ricky!

Carol Was the film good, Jane?

Jane The film? Oh, yes! It was brilliant, thanks!

3 Complete the questions with *was*, *were*, *had* or *went*. Then answer them.

1 Who _____ the only two cinema tickets?
2 Who _____ at the cinema first?
3 Who _____ across the street?
4 Who _____ into the cinema together?
5 Who _____ a really good time?

4 🗣 Work with a partner. Close your books and try to remember the whole story of 'Ricky the Spy'. Take turns to tell parts of the story again.

Review

The past simple tense of *be*, *have* and *go*

be
Two positive forms: *was*, *were*.
Negative forms: *wasn't* (*was not*) and *weren't* (*were not*).

I/he/she/it	was/wasn't
You (singular and plural)	were/weren't
We/they	were/weren't

have
One positive form: *had*.   Negative: *didn't + have*.
Questions: *did + have*?   *Did she have a holiday last year?*

go
One positive form: *went*.   Negative: *didn't + go*.
Questions: *Did + go*?   *Where did you go?*

Adverbs of past time

yesterday, last (night/week/Monday/July), in (May/June)

1 a   Make notes on these questions about yourself.

	Saturday 6.30 p.m.	Sunday 10.00 a.m.	Monday 7.15 a.m.
1 Where were you?			
2 Who were you with?			
3 What was the weather like?			
4 What clothes did you have on?			
5 Where did you go next, and at what times?			

b   Write full answers to the questions.

2 Ask your partner to check your report.

Vocabulary

Look at the unit again. Add all the new words for the weather, adjectives to describe feelings and past time adverbs to your vocabulary book.

Freewheeling ....

Test your memory.

a   A clever and dangerous spy is in town. Look at the things on the table in the spy's hotel room. Write six questions about the things.

Examples
What did the spy have on the table? What were some of the dates and times and places on the tickets?

b   Give your questions to another student, close your books and try to answer his/her questions.

Where was the spy on 6th May?

Lost and found

The past simple: regular verbs

Last summer there was a circus in our town. My sister, Alex, wanted to go – she's twelve – and my parents asked me to go with her. I didn't want to go, really, but I said yes …

CIRCUS

17th – 21st August at South Park

1 a 📖 Read these summaries of Gemma's story – only one is true.

1 They arrived at the circus quite late. There were no more tickets, so they went back to the bus-stop and waited a long time for the bus. Finally, the bus arrived but it went to the wrong place.

2 They had good seats at the circus, and they enjoyed the show. After the show Alex wanted a hamburger but Gemma wanted to go home. They had an argument. Then Gemma jumped on the first bus, without Alex.

3 They arrived at the circus but they missed the first part of the show. Alex didn't want to go in – she wanted to come back the next evening. Gemma agreed, so they went home again by bus.

b 📧 What happened to Gemma and Alex? Listen and choose the right summary.

Work it out: the past simple (4)

2 a Underline the regular past simple forms of *want* in Gemma's speech bubble. Complete the chart.

Present	Past simple
want	_____
don't want	_____

b Put the verbs in these sentences in the past simple.

1 Alex (want) to go to the circus.
2 Gemma (not want) to go to it, really.
3 They both (enjoy) the horses and the acrobats.
4 Alex (be) hungry. She (want) a hamburger.
5 Alex (jump) on another bus, twenty minutes later.

Pronunciation: *-ed* endings

3 We pronounce the *-ed* ending in three different ways.

a 📧 Listen and repeat.

1 /ɪd/ wanted   2 /t/ liked   3 /d/ enjoyed

b 📧 Listen to these verbs. Are the endings the same as 1 (wanted), 2 (liked) or 3 (enjoyed)? Write 1, 2 or 3 in the boxes.

arrived ☐   moved ☐   waited ☐
asked ☐   opened ☐   watched ☐
hoped ☐   started ☐

c Listen and repeat all the verbs.

4 👥 Work with a partner. Tell Gemma's story again.

5 📧 Listen to Gemma's story. Check your story. Was it the same?

What happened next?

waited/bus stop

then/went home

arrived/flat/open/door

message

after that/waited/two hours/tired

1 🗩 We use sequencing words (*first*, *then*, *next*, *after that*) to show the order of events in a story. Work with a partner.

A Look at the pictures. What happened after Gemma lost her sister? Tell the next part of the story using the words under the pictures.

B Turn to page 111. Read Gemma's diary about that evening and listen to A's story. Is A's story right?

2 What happened next? Choose an ending.

1 Gemma's parents telephoned. Alex was OK but she was in hospital.
2 Alex walked in without her parents. They were still at the airport!
3 Gemma's parents arrived home and Alex was with them. She was OK.

Useful English 📼

Showing interest

Really?   Go on …   What happened next?
Did they?

Sequencing words

first then next after that finally

3 🗩 Work with a partner. Work out the full story for your ending. Then tell it to two other students. Try to use some of the 'Useful English' phrases.

4 🗩 Work with a partner.

A You are Gemma's mother or father. Ask Gemma what happened.
Did you arrive home a long time ago?
Did you wait at the bus-stop?
Did you go to the police?
Did you call the airport?
Did you enjoy …?

B You are Gemma. Answer your parents' questions.
Yes, I did./No, I didn't.

5 Look at the questions in Exercise 4. Change these statements into *Did …?* questions.

1 She enjoyed the circus. *Did she enjoy the circus?*
2 They liked the horses.
3 They had an argument.
4 She arrived home at about 11 o'clock.
5 She called the police.

6 📖 Read the next page of Gemma's diary. Was your ending (Exercise 2) the same?

Finally, the door opened and my parents
walked in with Alex! They weren't angry
with me – I think they were angry with
Alex, really, but they were so happy that
she was safe, they didn't show it. I had
hundreds of questions, of course: Where
did she go? What happened? Why was
she at the airport? But she was really
tired and she didn't want to tell me the
story that night. My mother showed me
the police report about it.

In the news

Preparing newspaper reports

1 a 📼 Listen to these radio news reports. Match them with the newspaper headlines.

☐ **RAIN STOPS WIMBLEDON TENNIS AGAIN**

☐ **BOMB SEARCH AT CALIFORNIA THEME PARK**

☐ **GROUP OF HIJACKERS TAKE RUSSIAN PLANE**

☐ **PRESIDENT FINALLY DECIDES DOG'S NAME**

☐ **HERO OF THE UNDERSEA WORLD DIES**

b Check the meaning of any new words in the headlines. Use a dictionary.

2 a Listen again. Which reports mention these places?

    a Paris   report _____

    b Los Angeles   report _____

    c London   report _____

    d Moscow   report _____

    e Washington report _____

b Choose one of the news reports. Write a sentence or two to summarize what happened, and when.

Example
The American President finally decided the name for his family's new dog yesterday. The dog is called 'Buddy'.

3 📖 In the next day's newspapers there were new reports about the hijacking of the Russian plane. Only one of these three reports is correct – read them and guess which one.

1   Russian police last night stormed the hijacked plane at Moscow airport. They arrested the three hijackers – students from the University of Magadan, reports say. All the passengers and crew are safe.

2   The three hijackers of the Russian plane at Moscow airport last night decided to take the plane to Switzerland. Local TV news reported last night that the plane was in the air again, with all the 140 passengers still on board. Police say that the three men are extremely dangerous.

3   The hijacking of the Russian plane at Moscow airport ended in disaster last night, when the hijackers started to kill the passengers and crew one by one.

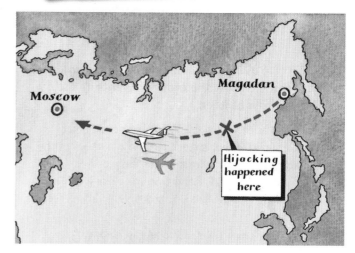

4 💬 Work in groups. Discuss and agree which report is the right one. What clues did you have from the cassette? Make a list.

5 📼 Listen and check your guess in Exercise 3.

Dictation

6 a 📻 Listen again and complete the radio news report.

Reports from ¹ _____ say that
² _____ police ³ _____ the hijacked
⁴ _____ at Moscow ⁵ _____ last night and
⁶ _____ the three ⁷ _____ of the plane. The three
men are ⁸ _____ from the ⁹ _____ of Magadan –
police cannot ¹⁰ _____ the reasons for the
¹¹ _____. All the ¹² _____ and ¹³ _____ are safe.

b Listen again. Check your dictation.

7 📖 Read the beginnings of two newspaper stories. Can you guess the endings? Use the pictures to help you.

A The Squid

Jean Grillette, 20, had an unusual accident in his open-top sports car near Toulon, France, three days ago. He was behind a van with boxes of squid in the back. The wind lifted a large squid out of one box and

B Brothers

In 1969 a young man from Newcastle, in the north of England, moved to live in Australia. Thirty years later, in 1999, he returned to England from Australia on holiday because he wanted to see his long-lost brother again. He went back to their old family home and asked about his brother. 'Oh no, he's not here now,' a woman there said. 'He went to

Writing: a story

8 ✏️ Work with a partner.

a Choose one newspaper report from Exercise 7.

b Write a plan for the story.

  A Make notes about what happened before the events in the newspaper story.
Who were the main people in the story? What were their jobs? Where were they immediately before the story? Why?

  B Make notes about what happened immediately after this. Think of a good ending.

c Practise telling the whole story with your partner, from your 'before' and 'after' notes.

d Tell your story to another pair of students. Listen to their story and ask them questions about it: *Who was/were …? When …?*

9 a ✏️ Write the whole of your story in no more than 120 words. Remember to use some sequencing words in your story.

b Swap your story with the same partner.

  1 Check the number of words.
  2 Check all the past simple verbs.

c Complete your story and write it out again.

Come on, Carol!

1 a Which five of these past simple verbs are in this episode, do you think? Look quickly at the pictures, but don't read the text. <u>Underline</u> the verbs.

arrived   crashed   damaged
decided to   died   filmed   helped
rescued   started to   worked

b 📼 Listen and read. Check your guesses.

1 | **That morning**

They went to the cinema together!

Dave I went to the cinema with Jane last night. That new film was really good.
Jack Oh, was it?

2 | **An hour later**

Jack Let's start. Dave, you wash the walls of the Coffee Corner. Then clean those brushes ... Then ...

Why am I getting all the dirty jobs?

Emma You're giving Dave all the really horrible jobs, Jack. That's not fair.

It's because of last night.

Jack OK, OK. I'm sorry.
Carol Ooh – my back!

3

Jack Have a break now, Dave. I can open those tins.
Dave OK. Thanks, Jack.
Jack What's the matter now!
Carol Er ... I've got a headache, Dave.
Emma Oh, look! The TV people are here.

4 The TV Producer and her cameraman arrived. They wanted to start filming the club members at work. And suddenly Carol's headache was all right. First she helped Emma to clean a wall. Then she helped Jack and Jane. After that she started to paint a wall! Carol worked really hard and the cameraman filmed her all day ...

Jane Great work, Carol! ... but there's quite a lot of paint on the floor. Can you come in early tomorrow and clean it up?

2 Use five of the verbs from Exercise 1 to write five questions in the past simple with *did*.

Examples
Did the TV people arrive at the club before they started work? When did the TV people arrive at the club?

3 🗣 Work with a partner. Ask your five questions. Take turns.

4 🗣 What do you think about Carol in this episode?

Review

The past simple: regular verbs

Positive   infinitive + -ed   *enjoyed, helped, started*
Negative   *didn't* + infinitive   *didn't want, didn't help*

The positive and negative forms are the same for all the pronouns.

Spelling rule: When the verb already ends in *-e*, only add *-d*. *liked, arrived, saved*

Sequencing words

These words and phrases make the order of events clear.
first … then … next … after that … finally …

1 Say the verbs below quietly to yourself. What is the pronunciation of the *-ed* ending? Write 1 for /ɪd/, 2 for /t/ or 3 for /d/.

closed [3]   listened [ ]   looked [ ]   opened [ ]

searched [ ]   stopped [ ]   wanted [ ]   walked [ ]

2 a Use the verbs in Exercise 1 to complete these sentences. Use one verb twice.

1 There was the safe, in one corner of the room. She _opened_ the door of the safe with the numbers from his diary.

2 She _____ inside the safe. Yes! His papers were all there.

3 She _____ carefully through the papers. She _____ that letter – she must have it! … Yes, this was it!

4 With the letter now in her hand, she _____ the door of the safe again quietly.

5 She _____ back across the room, _____ and _____ for a minute then she went out and _____ the door behind her.

b The sentences in Exercise 2a make a very short story. Add new details to the story. Answer these questions:

Who was the woman ('she')? Who was the man (the owner of the diary and the safe)? Where was the room, and where was the house it was in? What was in the letter? Why did she want it? What happened after she closed the door of the room?

c ✏ Write the complete story.

Vocabulary

Look at the unit again. Add all the new verbs for telling stories and making reports, and sequencing adverbs to your vocabulary book.

Freewheeling ....

Play 'Hangman'.

One student: You are 'the hangman'.
1 Choose a new word from this unit, for example, *acrobats*. Do not say what the word is.
2 On the board, draw lines for the number of letters in the word. *acrobats* = _ _ _ _ _ _ _ _

Other students:
1 Make two teams.
2 A student from one team guesses a letter: *T*.
3 If the letter *is* in the word, 'the hangman' writes the letter on the right line/s in the word:
_ _ _ _ _ _ *T* _
But if the letter is not in the word, or the guess is wrong, 'the hangman' draws the first line of a gallows for that team, like this:

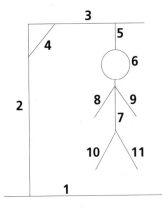

Behind the camera

The past simple: irregular verbs

1 a Look at the 'map'. Who was the director of these films? Guess.

b Check your guess with other students. Do you all agree?

2 🗫 Work in a group. Do you know any of the films in the 'map'? What can you say about them?

Who were the stars of these films? Were they good?
What was the main idea of the story?
Who did what? Where? Why?
Why do you think they were good or bad films?

3 📼 Listen and check your answer in Exercise 1. Match the dates and the facts about the director's life.

Dates	Facts
1947	He wrote and then made his first film with actors: *Escape to Nowhere*.
1959	He made *Jaws* and it immediately became an enormous hit.
1961	He won a Hollywood 'Oscar' for his film *Schindler's List*.
1968–70	His father gave him his first small movie camera and he made his first, very short film – about his toy trains.
1974–5	He was born in Cincinnati.
1994	He studied film-making at Long Beach College in California and made five short films.

Work it out: the past simple (5)

4 a Look at Exercise 3. Write the irregular past simple forms of these verbs.

	Verb	Past simple form
1	become	_____
2	give	_____
3	make	_____
4	win	_____
5	write	_____

b Write a list of the negative past simple forms of these verbs.

c Keep special pages for irregular verbs in your vocabulary book. Add new irregular verbs to your list when you meet them.

1 *Jaws* – the book

This is the terrifying story of Jaws. Peter Benchley wrote the book in 1973.

One night a young woman went for a swim in the sea near New York. A shark attacked and killed her. The police found only parts of her body. A few days later the killer fish came back and took a little boy from the same beach. His mother never saw him again.

The police chief, Martin Brody, asked for help. Quint, a local shark-hunter, knew what to do. Brody, Quint and a scientist called Hooper went out to hunt the shark. The shark killed Hooper and Quint, but Brody survived to tell the story of the fight against Jaws.

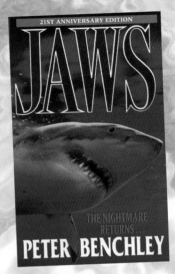

2 *Jaws* – the film

In 1974 Universal Studios asked Steven Spielberg to make a film from Benchley's story. Filming began in April 1974 on the north-east coast of the USA.

In October 1974 Verna Shields, the editor, and Spielberg started to edit the film in Los Angeles. On 20th June 1975 Jaws opened in 464 American cinemas. By 15th August it was in 954 cinemas. It made $14 million in its first week! By December 1977 that amount was $250 million.

---

5 Read the texts about *Jaws*. Find three interesting facts about the film – things that you did not know before.

6 a Look quickly through the two texts again. Which of these are names of real people and which are fictional people? Write *R* or *F*.

Quint ☐   Martin Brody ☐

Verna Shields ☐   Peter Benchley ☐

Hooper ☐   Steven Spielberg ☐

b Which text tells a real story and which one tells a fictional story?

7 Find other words or phrases in the two texts with the same or nearly the same meaning as:

1 frightening
2 shark
3 started

Learn to learn: taking notes

8 a What are the main facts in 'the film' text (2)? Make lists of:

   1 the important dates
   2 the names of places or areas
   3 the facts about cinemas
   4 the facts about money

b What facts can you find in 'the book' text (1)?

9 In the texts, find the positive forms of the verbs below. Complete the puzzle with them.

1 didn't find
2 didn't see
3 didn't write
4 didn't take
5 didn't come
6 didn't attack
7 didn't know
8 didn't begin

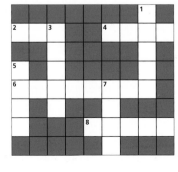

The world of silence

1 👓 Work with a partner. Look at the photo and try to answer the questions about it.

1 Which famous city is this man in?
2 The man died in 1997, but what did he do during his life? Was he …
   a a writer?   d an environmentalist?
   b an explorer?   e an inventor?
   c a film-maker?
3 Look at the title at the top of this page. Where or what is 'the world of silence'? Guess.
4 Do you know the man's name?

2 📖 Read the text.

a Check and correct your guesses.

b Find the past simple forms of these verbs.

   1 read   3 say   5 understand
   2 speak   4 think   6 fight

c Add the new verbs to the lists of irregular verbs in your vocabulary book.

3 Match the five paragraphs of the text with these headings.

a his film-making and writing ___
b his different types of work and interests ___
c his great invention ___
d his death ___
e his environmental work ___

The old man of the sea

1 Underwater explorer Jacques Cousteau died yesterday in Paris at the age of 87. His environmental organization, The Cousteau Society, said: 'Jacques Cousteau returned yesterday to the world of silence'. *The World of Silence* is the title of his great film about life under the sea. 🗸□

2 The French film-maker was also famous for his television programmes, *The Undersea World of Jacques Cousteau* – films about his adventures on his ship, the *Calypso*. 🗸□

An aqualung

He was also famous for exploring, filming and writing books about sea plants and animals.

3 Cousteau fought all through his life for the environment. In 1995, for example, he was strongly against France's nuclear tests in the Pacific Ocean.

4 He was also an inventor. In 1943 he invented the aqualung with another Frenchman, Emile Gagnan. 🗸□

5 He had many interests. He was an explorer and adventurer, a writer and film-maker, an inventor and businessman. He spoke French, English and German fluently, understood Spanish and read Russian. 🗸□ He was a hero of modern France. He took us into worlds we never knew or thought about before.

4 Read the text again and find these facts about Cousteau.

1 How old was he when he died?
2 What was the name of his environmental organization?
3 What was the date of his famous invention?
4 What languages did he speak fluently?
5 What languages did he only understand or read?

5 a Find the best place to add these new pieces of information to the text. Write the number of the sentence next to the right place in the text.

Example (in paragraph 2)

… films about his adventures on his ship, the *Calypso*. ⋏ **1**

1 The ship sank in an accident in 1996.
2 He won the top prize at the Cannes Film Festival for this film in 1956.
3 He was also a good piano-player, a poet and a painter in his free time.
4 This invention gave divers a way to stay under water and move around freely for long periods of time, with their own oxygen on their backs.

b Compare your answers with other students.

Jobs and hobbies

Vocabulary: jobs

1 Look at the text again. Circle the different types of work and interests that Cousteau had.

2 📖 Read the clues and match them with the jobs in the box. Check new words in your dictionary.

architect	doctor	farmer	film-star
lawyer	politician	secretary	

1 She looked carefully into my eyes and mouth. Then she told me I was not ill.
2 He promised us more jobs, more money, more free time – and we believed **him**!
3 His boss, Ms Take, told him to bring **her** the letters immediately. He was late, she said.
4 There were terrible things about her in the newspapers the next day. Critics – she *hated* **them**!
5 My father and I went to see him and he talked to **us** about the date for going to court.
6 'I sent you the plan for your new office last week. Didn't you get **it**?'

3 Look at the sentences in Exercise 2 again.

1 In sentence 2, who is 'him'? _____
2 In sentence 3, who is 'her'? _____
3 In sentence 4, who is 'them'? _____
4 In sentence 5, who is 'us'? _____
5 In sentence 6, what is 'it'? _____

Writing: a famous person

4 🖊 Would you like to do any of the things Cousteau did? What job/jobs do you want to do in the future?

a Choose one famous person who has (or had) an interesting job. Discuss what you know about him or her. Write some facts about your person and his/her job.

b Organize your notes into sentences. Use all the facts you have. Use some of the past simple forms you know. Look back at the texts to help you.

Example

He was born in September 1976.
He was born near Rio de Janeiro in Brazil.
He became a footballer in …
Now he plays for … etc.

c 🗪 Work in groups. Ask questions about other students' famous people. Answer questions about your famous person.

Chocolate chip cookies

1 a Look at the pictures for one minute, only. Do not read the text. Cover the pictures and choose five of these verbs which you think are in the story. Underline them.

ate	came	fought	left
made	read	sank	saw	sat
sent	spoke	told	won

b What are the infinitives of the five verbs you underlined?

c 🔲 Listen and read. Check your answers.

1

Jane Let's meet here at nine tomorrow, Carol. We can clean up before the others get here. OK?
Carol Yes, sure, Jane. See you tomorrow.

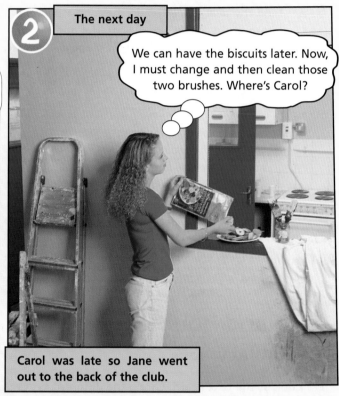

2 The next day

We can have the biscuits later. Now, I must change and then clean those two brushes. Where's Carol?

Carol was late so Jane went out to the back of the club.

3

Carol arrived at 9.15. She didn't start to clean up … Instead, she sat down, read a magazine and ate all the biscuits! Then Carol looked at her watch again. Jane still wasn't there! Carol decided to change into her work clothes.

4

Ricky Hey! Who ate all the chocolate chip cookies? They're my favourite biscuits.
Jane I don't know. I left a new packet there …

Mmm. Where's Carol? She came before me … and they're *her* favourite biscuits too.

2 a Which of these adjectives can you use to describe Carol in this part of the story? Use your dictionary, if necessary.

> annoyed   friendly   greedy   hungry
> interesting   late   lazy   helpful   pleased   tidy

b Write pairs of sentences about Carol with the adjectives you chose, then join the sentences together with the word *because*.

Example
Carol didn't start work. She was lazy.
Carol didn't start work because she was lazy.

3 🗨 Work in groups. What do you think about the things Carol did at the club that morning? Why? Discuss it together.

Review

The past simple: irregular verbs

This unit introduces some common irregular verbs. There are a lot of irregular verbs in English.

Object pronouns (see also page 47)

Look at these sentences.

1 *Susan* found *the money* under a chair.
2 *She* found *it* under a chair.
   (*She* – subject pronoun, *it* – object pronoun)

The object pronouns are:

Singular	Plural
me	us
you	you
him/her/it	them

1 Find the positive past simple forms of these verbs in this unit and add them to your vocabulary book, if necessary.

> be   become   begin   come   do   eat
> fight   find   give   go   have   know
> leave   make   read   say   see   send
> sink   sit   speak   take   tell   think
> understand   write   win

2 Change the <u>underlined</u> words into pronouns.

1 <u>Cousteau</u> was 87 years old when he died.
2 <u>Carol</u> asked <u>the other members of the club</u> to listen to her.
3 <u>Spielberg</u> began working on <u>a new film</u> last month.
4 <u>Jack and Emma</u> sat behind <u>Jane</u> on the train.
5 <u>My sister</u> gave some cinema tickets to <u>my friend and me</u>.

Vocabulary

Look at the unit again. Add all the new words for films and jobs to your vocabulary book.

Freewheeling ....

a 📼 Listen and complete the song with words from the box.

> came   crowd   fingers   found   had
> heard (x2)   life (x2)   read   sang   was

Strumming my pain with his ———
Singing my ——— with his words
Killing me softly with his song
Killing me softly with his song
Telling my whole ——— with his words
Killing me softly with his song …

I ——— he ——— a good song
I ——— he ——— a style
And so I ——— to see him
And listened for a while
And there he ———, this young boy
A stranger to my eyes

Chorus

I felt all flushed with fever
Embarrassed by the ———
I felt he ——— my letters
And ——— each one out loud
I prayed that he would finish
But he just kept right on …

b Listen again. Check your answers and sing the song. What do you think the title of the song is? Guess.

c Find three more irregular verbs in the song. Add them to your vocabulary book.

Great journeys

Sequences of events

1 Look at the photograph. Where are the explorers? What is different about these explorers? Guess.

28th May 1997

At the top of the world

Four British explorers arrived at the North Pole early this morning. They were the first all-women team of explorers to walk there. When they arrived, they waited for the plane to come later that day with their friends and relatives. They are staying in the Arctic for another six days, then they are coming back to Britain on 3rd June.

The 700-kilometre walk started two months ago on 14th March. There were five teams of four women. Each team walked over 100 kilometres in freezing weather. They pulled all their food and equipment behind them. The last team began their walk ten days ago and completed it at 5.45 this morning.

Caroline Hamilton, one of the explorers, started to organize the expedition two years ago. Then, in September last year, she chose 20 women for her team. They trained and planned the trip for the next six months. Then they were ready for a really amazing experience.

2 📖 Read the article quickly and check your answers to Exercise 1.

3 Read the article again, carefully. When did these things happen? Put them in the right order. Write 1–7 in the boxes. Then write the date for each event.

	Event	Order	When (date, etc.)
A	The last group arrived at the North Pole.	☐	_28/5/97_
B	Their friends and relatives arrived.	☐	_____
C	The last team came back to Britain.	☐	_____
D	The long walk across the Arctic began.	☐	_____
E	The last group started their part of the walk.	☐	_____
F	The organizers chose twenty women for the team.	_1_	_____
G	The team trained and planned the expedition.	☐	_____

4 Write the events of the expedition in the right order. Use the sentences from Exercise 3 and sequencing words: *first, then, next …*

Example
First, the organizers chose 20 women for the team. Then the women trained and …

Vocabulary

5 The word *explorer* is a noun. It comes from the verb *explore*. Find nouns for these verbs.

1 explore
2 teach
3 produce TV programmes
4 write books
5 invent things
6 work in science
7 work in business
8 use a TV camera

Example
explore → *explorer*

Talking about the future

1 🔊 Hundreds of years ago, explorers travelled the Silk Road, from the Mediterranean to China. Now Roger and a group of his friends are planning an expedition for later this year. They are walking part of the old Silk Road. Listen to Roger. On the map, tick the towns you hear and write the dates.

2 a Listen again and complete the questions.

1 When are you _____?

2 Are you _____ the walk immediately?

3 Where are you _____ on the way?

4 Are you _____ back from Bukhara?

5 Are you _____ a lot of preparation at the moment?

6 Are you _____ about the area too?

b 🗣 Work with a partner. Listen again.

A Make notes of the answers to questions 1, 3 and 5.

B Make notes of the answers to questions 2, 4 and 6.

c Ask and answer the questions.

B Ask questions 1, 3 and 5.

A Ask questions 2, 4 and 6.

Work it out:
the present continuous with future meaning

3 a Look at sentences 1 and 2.

1 I'm staying with my sister at the moment.

2 I'm staying at the Hilton Hotel next week.

These two present continuous sentences have different meanings. Write 1 or 2 in the boxes.

the future ☐   the present ☐

Which words helped you to complete the boxes?

b Complete these sentences with *at the moment* or *next week*.

1 I'm starting at my new school _____.

2 I'm studying history at school _____. It's difficult!

3 It's really hot. They're working at home _____ because the office hasn't got windows.

4 We're going to the museum _____.

c Look at the questions in Exercise 2. Write *P* (for present) or *F* (for future) next to them.

4 🗣 Work with a partner. Ask and answer about your plans for the weekend and find a time to meet.

A What are you doing on Friday evening?

B I'm going to the cinema with some friends. What are you doing on Saturday morning?

Pronunciation: /w/ and /v/

5 a 🔊 Look at this phrase and listen: *we're leaving*. Repeat the /w/ and /v/ sounds: <u>we</u>'re lea<u>v</u>ing.

b 🔊 Listen and write the words. Then tick the sounds you hear for each word.

		/w/	/v/
1	leaving		✓
2			
3			
4			
5			
6			
7			

On the town

1 Do you know anything about London? What can you find in London (or other big cities)?

Vocabulary: places in a town

2 Match the places in Column A with the things you can see or find there (Column B).

	A	B
1	a gallery	actors and musicians
2	a market	an important family
3	a palace	pictures
4	a theatre	animals
5	a wax museum	food, clothes to buy
6	a zoo	models of famous people

3 Find examples of some of the places from Exercise 2 in the pictures and on the map.

4 a 📼 Alison wants to go to London on Saturday. Listen to her phone call with Luke and write their plans for Saturday.

Example
Alison is doing some shopping in the morning.

b What time can they meet to go to London?

5 a 📼 Listen to some information about places in London. Complete the 'open' and 'closes' columns of the chart.

b Listen again and complete the 'Time for visit' column.

	Opens	Closes	Time for visit
Buckingham Palace	9.30	4.15	two hours
The London Dungeon			
London Zoo			
Madame Tussaud's			
Rock Circus			
The Tower of London			

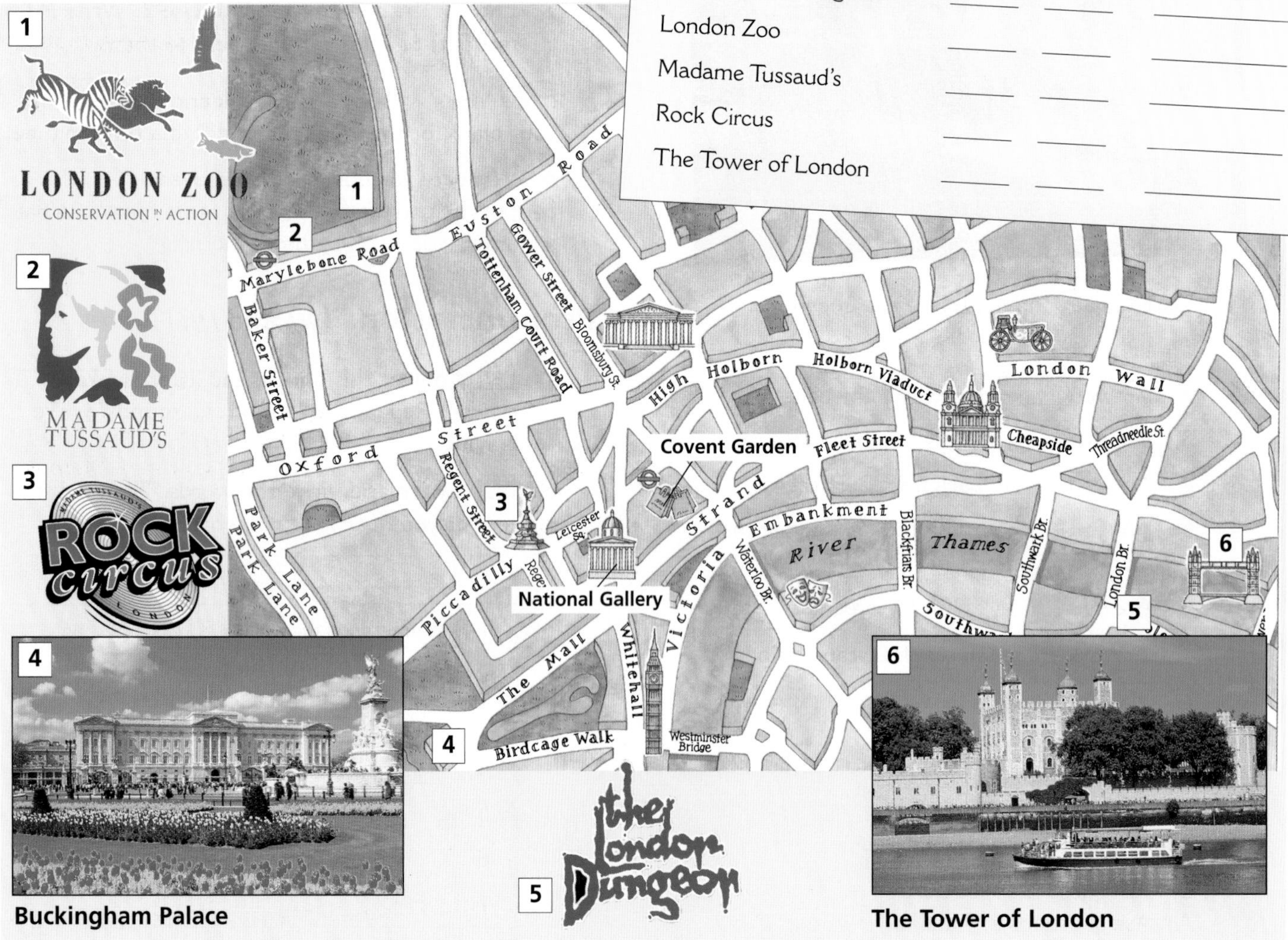

1 LONDON ZOO CONSERVATION IN ACTION

2 MADAME TUSSAUD'S

3 ROCK Circus

4

Buckingham Palace

6

The Tower of London

5 the London Dungeon

6 a Work in groups. Where can Alison and her friends go? How many places can they visit?

b Listen and check your answers. What are they doing on Saturday?

Work it out: making suggestions

7 a Look at these ways of making suggestions from the dialogue.

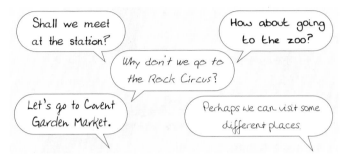

Shall we meet at the station?

How about going to the zoo?

Why don't we go to the Rock Circus?

Let's go to Covent Garden Market.

Perhaps we can visit some different places.

b Add them to the chart in the correct places.

Shall we _____	go out for the day?
_____ _____	go out for the day.
_____	going out for the day?

Useful English

Yes, good idea!
Great idea!   Oh no! I hate …
Yes, why not!   Sorry, but I'm …
Yes, I love …

Pronunciation: sentence stress

8 a Listen to the suggestions from the dialogue again. Underline the stressed words.

1 <u>Shall</u> we <u>meet</u> at the <u>station</u>?
2 How about going to the zoo?
3 Let's go to Covent Garden Market.
4 Perhaps we can visit some different places.
5 Why don't we go to the Rock Circus?

b Listen and repeat the sentences.

c Work with a partner. Practise making the suggestions above and answering them.

9 Work in groups. You have one day in London and you want to visit some places. You can visit only three places. Use all the information on these pages to plan your day together. Remember to use suggestions.

Example
A *Shall we go to Madame Tussaud's?*
B *Good idea.*

Writing: plans

10 You received this letter from your penfriend yesterday.

> Thanks for your invitation to visit you next month for a weekend. Mum and Dad agreed, so we went to a travel agent's yesterday and booked the trip! I'm arriving on Friday 23rd at 12.20 (midday) and I'm leaving on Monday 26th at 2.30, so I must be at the bus station at 2.00. I hope that's OK.

a Make a list of interesting places in and near your town. Then plan the visit.

Example
Friday afternoon: go to the …
Friday evening: pizza at …

b Write about your plans.

c Check your writing.

Are you using the present continuous for your plans? Check your days and times.

d Write a letter to your penfriend. Here is the start and the ending for you.

> Dear …
> We're happy that you're coming to visit us next weekend. These are our plans for the weekend.
> On Friday afternoon we're …
>
> Best wishes (Write your name)

Plans for a party

1 **a** The members of the OK Club are having a party. What are their plans? Guess. Complete this word-map about parties.

Food   Drinks

Party

Music   Other things

b 📼 Listen and read. Are the members of the club doing the things in your word-map?

① Jane So *who* came in and ate all the cookies?
Carol I did. I'm sorry. I was really hungry, that's all.
Dave Well, you can go out and buy another bag for us.

② Later that morning

Jack We've still got about £58 from Project OK. What do you want to do with it?
Emma You're a great project boss, Jack! Let's have a party.
Ricky Yes, that's a great idea!

③ Half an hour later

Ricky I asked my parents. They're making some Caribbean food for us.
Emma My brother's bringing some huge pizzas for us.
Dave Our Mum is making some cakes.
Carol Does she *know* that, Dave?

④ Jane Hey! The TV people are coming to film us!

Emma Wow! What can I wear?
Jane Well, I'm just wearing jeans and a new blouse. I can't dance in a skirt, and I really want to dance!
Jack What are you wearing, Ricky?
Ricky My new waistcoat from Jamaica. It's really cool!

2 What are the plans? Who is doing what for the party? Write sentences.

Example
Emma's brother is bringing some pizzas.

1	Emma's brother	making a film of the party
2	The TV people	making some Caribbean food
3	Dave and Carol's mother	bringing some pizzas
4	Ricky's parents	making some cakes

3 🗪 Work with a partner. Make suggestions for a party and answer them.

Example
make a list of all the people we want to ask
A *Let's make a list of the people we want to ask.*
B *Yes, I think that's a great idea./No. That's a terrible idea!*

1 play some party games
2 have a fashion competition
3 have a disco dancing competition
4 have a barbecue
5 ask everyone to come in unusual clothes

Review

Present continuous with future meaning

There are two common uses of the present continuous in English:

1 to talk about the present
What are you doing, Dad?
I'm washing the car (now/today/at the moment).

2 to talk about future plans
What are you doing at the weekend?
We're visiting friends in London tomorrow, and we're going to a party on Sunday.

Making suggestions

We can make suggestions in different ways:

	+ infinitive
Shall we … Why don't we …	have a pizza?
Perhaps we can … Let's …	have a pizza.
	+ *-ing* form
How about …	having a pizza?

1 This is Emma's diary for next week. Write sentences about her week.

Example
Emma's taking a French test at two o'clock on Monday.

2 🗪 Work with a partner. You are on holiday in London and you want to go out tomorrow evening. Use these adverts to make suggestions, and decide where you are going tomorrow evening.

Vocabulary

Look at the unit again. Add all the new words about travel, places in a town, and time phrases to your vocabulary book.

Freewheeling ....

Where do I work?

Play this game in groups of four. Take turns.

A	Think of a place in your town. Write it in your notebook. Do not tell the other students.
B, C and D	Ask *yes/no* questions to find out where A works.

Examples
Is it a big place? Do you work outside? Do you wear special clothes? Do people buy things from you?

Can you find out with only ten questions?

15 Losing things

1 a Do you lose things at school or in town? What sort of things do people often lose? Make a list.

   b Compare your list with other students' lists.

   c What happens when you lose something at school, and another person finds it? Is there a lost property box or person at your school?

   d What is *lost property* in your language?

2 a 📖 Read the text. Find two places where people often lose things in London.

   b Where is the Lost Property Office?

Every day people lose things on buses and underground trains in London. Some of the things they lose are very unusual. On one famous occasion a young man left a human skeleton on a bus, for example! Why was he on a bus with a skeleton? The story is a mystery, but it is absolutely true.

People usually lose things they are carrying with them, for example an umbrella, a book or a camera. The Lost Property Office in Baker Street has dozens of these every year. Sometimes people lose things from their pockets, such as wallets or purses, or a pair of glasses. Small things easily fall out of coat or trouser pockets.

But how can you lose your false teeth? The Lost Property Office has a box of lost false teeth! And how can you lose large things, musical instruments, for example, or babies' push-chairs, or a stuffed animal or bird? The Lost Property Office gets things like these every year.

100

3 a In the text, find examples of three different types of lost property.

   1 things people often have in their pockets
   2 small things people carry
   3 large or unusual things

b How many of the things in the text and the photos did you have on your list (Exercise 1a)? Add any new words to your vocabulary book.

4 📼 Listen to three phone calls to a lost property office. Which of the things in the picture are the people looking for? Write the letters of the three things.

Phone call 1 ___   Phone call 2 ___   Phone call 3 ___

Offers

Useful English 📼

Offers	Answers
Can I help you?	Yes, please. Thanks!
I'll (have it ready) for you.	Thank you very much.
Shall I (take your name)?	No, thank you. It's OK.
Let me (take your name).	It's all right, thanks.

1 a Complete the phone call to a lost property office. Use the 'Useful English' phrases.

Woman   Hello. Manchester Lost Property

           Office. _____?

Man   _____. I lost my wallet

           and two credit cards on the 316 bus

           yesterday.

Woman   _____ your name and

           _____ if _____

           is here.

Man   _____.

b 📼 Listen and check your answers.

c 🗣 Work with a partner. Practise the dialogue and make new dialogues with the other 'Useful English' phrases and lost things.

2 🗣 Work with a partner. This morning you were both on a bus and you lost one of the things in the pictures.

a Prepare the situation. Who are you? What did you lose?

Situations
actors travelling to a film studio
friends going to a club
students travelling to/from art/medical school
brothers/sisters buying a birthday present in a city
brothers/sisters with your family on holiday
friends helping another friend to move house

b Prepare the details of your story. Discuss your ideas and make notes to answer these questions.

Which bus were you on?
Where did you get on the bus?
Were there other people on the bus? How many?
Where did you get off the bus?
When did you realize that you hadn't got your property?
What is your property and what does it look like?

c Check your story together carefully.

Finding your lost property

3 a 🗣 Find your property.
Pair A
Tell your story to the class. Answer their questions about the details of your story. Make the story as interesting as possible.
Class
You work at the lost property office. Listen to Pair A's story and ask questions about it. Use the questions in Exercise 2b to help you.

Examples
B *What are you doing with a video camera?*
A *We're art students, and we're making a film.*
B *How do we know it's your camera? Has it got your name on it?*

b Is the lost property really theirs? Take a class vote.

Humphrey, don't jump. Your briefcase is at the Lost Property Office.

More mix-ups

Possessive pronouns

1 a Look at the pictures of the bowling alley.
Complete the speech bubbles with the right
possessive pronouns.

mine	ours
yours	yours
his	theirs
hers	

b 📼 Listen and check your answers.

2 Listen again. Match the two parts of the sentences.

1 The white shoes are   (Nusrat's and Prya's) theirs
2 The blue shoes are   (Anna's and Bella's) theirs
3 The black shoes are   (Katy's) hers
4 The red shoes are   (Joe's) his

Work it out: possessive pronouns

3 Complete the questions and answers.

Questions: _____ is it? (Who does it belong to?)

_____ are they? (Who do they belong to?)

Answers: It's *my* bag. It's _____.

It's _____ jacket. It's *yours*.

They're *her* shoes. They're _____.

That's _____ book. It's *his*.

This is *our* classroom. It's _____.

That's *their* house. That's _____.

4 🗪 Play a game in a group. Collect together things from the people in your group, mix them, then play.

A Is this yours? … his? … hers?

B Yes, it is/No, it isn't. It's hers/his/theirs, etc.

You can only have your property back when you answer *Yes*.

one and *ones*

1 📖 Read the text. Put two pieces of information from it into the chart.

One day, Bella took her dog to a park. Two other women, Carol and Amy, were also in the park with their dogs. The three dogs all saw a cat and they ran after it and disappeared. The police found the dogs later and took them to a dogs' home. All the dogs were small and brown.

The man at the Dogs' Home put them into three cages: A, B and C. He gave them some food: dog-biscuits, dog food from a tin, and a bone. The one in Cage A only ate the dog-biscuits.

The one in Cage B didn't eat dog-biscuits or dog food from a tin. It only wanted the bone!

The one in Cage C ate the dog-food from a tin and some dog-biscuits. Later, the three dog owners phoned the Dogs' Home and asked about their missing pets. One woman lived in New Drive and one lived in Atlanta Avenue. The owner of the other dog, Bella, lived in Station Street.

Which dog belonged to which owner?

Owner's names			Amy
Where they live	Station Street		
What the dogs ate for dinner		Dog food from a tin and biscuits	
Cage (A, B, or C)			

2 📼 Listen to the three phone calls. Complete the rest of the chart and solve the problem.

3 🗪 Work with a partner. Check the information. Take turns to ask questions.

Example

A *Which one was Amy's?*

B *Hers was the one in Cage …*

Work it out: -*'s* or -*s'* (review)

4 Look at the rules. Then complete the sentences.
Rules:

1 -*'s* shows possession with singular nouns or people's names.

2 -*'s* shows possession with irregular plural nouns.

3 -*s'* shows possession with regular plural nouns.

1 The man at the Dog___ Home gave them dinner.

2 Whose dog is that? It's Carol___ dog.

3 The three women___ names are Amy, Bella and Carol.

4 Amy___ dog is brown and white.

5 The three dog___ names are 'Buster'.

Pronunciation: /s/, /ʃ/ and /z/

5 a 📼 Listen and repeat.

b Say the tongue-twister quickly.

She shows Sara's size six shoes to Sheila and Susan.

The OK Club on TV!

1 **a** 💬 Work in groups. Look at the title of this part of the story. Who is on TV? Where are they? What are they doing in the TV film? Look quickly at the pictures and make guesses. Discuss your ideas together.

b 📼 Listen and read. Check your guesses.

1 The morning after the party

Carol That was a wonderful party! Ricky's Jamaican waistcoat was really cool!
Jane Yes, you danced with him and his waistcoat three times!
Emma Let's go and clean up. The TV people are coming this afternoon to show us their video.

2

Jack Here ... let me give you a hand with that.
Dave Thanks, Jack.

3 That afternoon

Now we'll show you our film. Shall I start?

Emma Whose hand is that in front of the camera?
Carol Mine, I think.
Ricky There's Jack with *another* plate of food!

4

Carol And there's Dave, dancing with Jane – *again*!
Jane We danced together five times. He's a really good dancer. And Dave and I are going to the cinema again tomorrow ... without you, Ricky!

2 ✏️ After showing the video, the TV Producer and her cameraman are leaving. Write the last part of the story in your notebooks.

3 a 💬 Work in groups. Look at the titles of the 15 parts of the story. Can you remember the whole story? Can you tell it? Don't look back. Take turns to tell one part of the story each.

1	Pleased to meet you	9	Detective work
2	Help! Fire!	10	The trick
3	What a mess!	11	Ricky the spy
4	Emma's idea	12	Come on, Carol!
5	Hamburgers	13	Chocolate chip cookies
6	The people from TV 4	14	Plans for a party
7	Project OK	15	The OK club on TV!
8	Where's the money?		

b Which parts of the story did you enjoy most? Why? Talk about it together and look back at the whole story.

Review

Possessive pronouns

mine   yours   his   hers   its   ours   yours   theirs

Question: *Whose …?* (= Who does it belong to?)
Answer: *It's …* + possessive pronoun
'*Whose is this cassette?*' '*It's mine.*'

one or *ones*

We use *one* (singular) or *ones* (plural) when we do not want to repeat the same noun again and again.
'*Which street?*' '*The next one.*' (one = street)
'*Which tomatoes?*' '*The red ones.*' (ones = tomatoes)

1 Underline the right possessive pronoun or adjective to complete the sentences.

1   Those aren't *our/ours* books. The ones on the floor are *our/ours*.
2   Here are *yours/your* cassettes. Are the ones on the table *yours/your*, too?
3   That terrible man isn't *my/mine* husband. I can't see *my/mine*.
4   This isn't *hers/her* car. *Her/Hers* is green.
5   That isn't *their/theirs* house. *Their/Theirs* is the next one, I think.

2 Write this dialogue again with *one* or *ones* in the right places.

A   Hello. Can I help you?
B   Yes. I'd like an ice cream, please.
A   Which _____ would you like?
B   A banana _____, please.
A   Sorry, we haven't got any banana _____ left.
B   Which _____ have you got, then?
A   We've got strawberry _____ and chocolate _____.
B   Can I have a chocolate _____, please?

Vocabulary

Look at the unit again. Make a list of the possessive pronouns in your vocabulary book and add the new words for personal property and offers.

Freewheeling

Can you remember?

a   Look at the main picture on page 100 again for one minute. Try to remember the English words for all the things in the picture, and where they are.

b   Close your book. Write a list of all the things in the picture. Where are they?

Example
The wallet is between the bracelet and the video camera. / The wallet is next to the video camera.

c   Check your ideas with other students. Then look at the picture again.

Consolidation

Grammar

1 📖 Read the newspaper article about Kevin and complete it with verbs from the box. Use the past simple, present simple or present continuous.

> be   be (negative)   do   hear   know (negative)
> learn   leave   look   meet   put   run   ~~rescue~~
> say   see   stay   think   want   ~~win~~

Local hero!

Local boy Kevin Daley, 15, ¹ _won_ an award last week for bravery. Kevin ² _rescued_ Amy Warren, 8, from a beach near Poole, Dorset. Amy ³ _____ lost. Kevin was on a walk with a group of school friends when, luckily for Amy, he ⁴ _____ the path because he ⁵ _____ to look at a bird. When he went back to the path, his friends ⁶ _____ anywhere around. After a few minutes he ⁷ _____ a sound from the beach below. When he ⁸ _____ down, he ⁹ _____ a little girl, alone on the beach.

The police ¹⁰ _____ Amy on a train to London, where Amy's parents ¹¹ _____ her, happy to see their daughter again.
After his experience, Kevin ¹² _____, 'I ¹³ _____ where my friends went; I ¹⁴ _____ they ¹⁵ _____ away from me! That was lucky for Amy! My friends and I ¹⁶ _____ another walk next weekend, but this time I ¹⁷ _____ with them!'
Kevin ¹⁸ _____ how to read a map now!

2 a The article doesn't tell us about Kevin's rescue. Put these pictures about the rescue in the right order.

b Write one sentence for each picture. Use some sequencing words and these words.

> carry   cave   chocolate   cliff   climb   dark
> frightened   make a fire   path   policeman
> sleep   upset   water

3 📼 Listen to Kevin talking about his rescue of the little girl and check your answers.

4 a 💬 Work with a partner. Kevin is now famous! Everyone wants to talk to him.

    A You are Kevin. Next week you are giving a radio interview on Monday evening. You are meeting a local actor on Saturday morning. Write six more plans in your diary. Then answer your friend's questions.

    B You are Kevin's friend. Turn to page 111.

	Morning	Afternoon	Evening
Monday	School	School	
Tuesday	School	School	
Wednesday	School	School	
Thursday	School	School	
Friday	School	School	
Saturday			
Sunday			

b Talk to your partner. Find a time to meet.

Example
    B Kevin, how about meeting on Monday evening?
    A No, I can't. I'm giving a radio interview. How about Tuesday evening?

Vocabulary

1 Complete this word-map with the weather anagrams.

arcle   dwiny   ewt   nair   morts   nusyn
~~onphoty~~   swon   wram

Weather
good weather   bad weather
    typhoon

2 Match the situations with the adjectives.

How do you feel when …
1	you're going on holiday tomorrow?	embarrassed
2	you can't go out with your friends?	excited
3	you make a silly mistake in class?	hungry
4	you didn't sleep well last night?	miserable
5	you want a drink?	tired
6	you want some food?	thirsty

3 Find eleven more places in this word-square.

```
G A L L E R Y  X G H
D R Y B X E F  K Y O
P Z M M U S E  U M S
A T H E A T R  E C T
R C Z T Y A L  P H E
K I K G J U Z  O O L
U N I V E R S  I T Y
S E P A L A C  E E T
L M V T Q N S  N L C
M A R K E T B  A N K
```

4 Look at units 11–15 again. Check that all the new words are in your vocabulary book. Look at your Workbook pages 73–76 and add any new words to the charts.

Communication

1 a Complete this conversation. Put one or more words in each gap. Make guesses if necessary.

    A Hello. 720 1364.
    D Hi, Angie. It's Dave here.
    A Dave! Wow! I last saw you **three years ago**! How are you?
    D I'm just ¹_____, Angie. Great. ²_____?
    A Oh, I'm fine. But, Dave, where are you? Why are you calling ³_____?
    D Well, Angie, I'm at home in **Boston** right now, but I've got a new job! I'm a ⁴_____ now, and guess what! I'm coming to England for a **concert** next ⁵_____!
    A That's **fantastic**! You were always ⁶_____ on the guitar. Where are you ⁷_____?
    D At the Kensington Park Hotel, in London.
    A Oh, nice. **How about meeting** one day?
    D Yes, **I'd like that**.
    A What are your plans?
    D Well, I'm working in the **studio from Wednesday to Friday**. I'm taking the plane back on **Sunday**, so ⁸_____ meet on **Saturday**?
    A OK. What shall we do?
    D Mmm. Let me think. I know. ⁹_____ take a **boat on the River Thames**?
    A Great idea! Then **let's have lunch** in Greenwich.
    D Perhaps we can go to a show in the evening.
    A Yes, I'd love that.

b 📼 Now listen. Are your answers the same as the cassette?

2 💬 Work with a partner. Make a new dialogue. Change the words in **bold**.

Project: a tourist guide

1 Look at the map below. It is a map of Covent Garden, an area of London. What can you remember about Covent Garden from Unit 14?

Listening

2 📼 Listen to the dialogues. Write the names of these places on the correct labels on the map.

Costa   Covent Garden Market   Tesco Metro   Sofra
The London Transport Museum   The Sanctuary

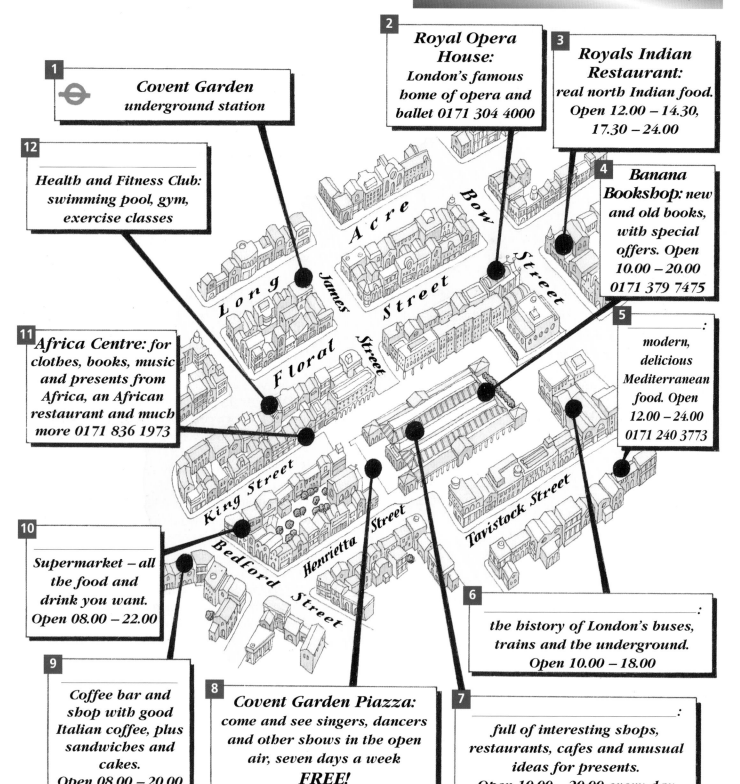

1 *Covent Garden* underground station

2 *Royal Opera House:* London's famous home of opera and ballet 0171 304 4000

3 *Royals Indian Restaurant:* real north Indian food. Open 12.00 – 14.30, 17.30 – 24.00

4 *Banana Bookshop:* new and old books, with special offers. Open 10.00 – 20.00 0171 379 7475

5 _____: *modern, delicious Mediterranean food. Open 12.00 – 24.00 0171 240 3773*

6 _____: *the history of London's buses, trains and the underground. Open 10.00 – 18.00*

7 _____: *full of interesting shops, restaurants, cafes and unusual ideas for presents. Open 10.00 – 20.00 every day*

8 *Covent Garden Piazza:* come and see singers, dancers and other shows in the open air, seven days a week **FREE!**

9 *Coffee bar and shop with good Italian coffee, plus sandwiches and cakes. Open 08.00 – 20.00*

10 *Supermarket – all the food and drink you want. Open 08.00 – 22.00*

11 *Africa Centre:* for clothes, books, music and presents from Africa, an African restaurant and much more 0171 836 1973

12 *Health and Fitness Club: swimming pool, gym, exercise classes*

Long   Acre   Bow   Street   James   Floral   Street   King Street   Bedford   Street   Henrietta   Street   Tavistock Street

Reading

3 Look at the map and the labels quickly. Answer each question with the number of a label.

1 Where can you have an Indian meal? ☐

2 Where can you buy something from Egypt or Zimbabwe? ☐

3 Where can you buy cheap books? ☐

4 Where can you see a show in the street? ☐

4 Read this text about one of the places on the map.

a Which place does the text describe?

> *The _____ moved into an old flower market on the east side of the piazza in the 1970s, when the old Covent Garden Market moved to another part of London. Here you can see the history of the capital's famous transport system, from the time when the river was the main transport to the underground trains of today. There's a lot for children to do. They can 'drive' a London bus and can explore all the different kinds of trains from the past.*
>
> *There's also an exhibition of London Transport posters, a shop and a cafe.*
>
> *Open from 10 a.m. – 6 p.m. every day, £3.95. Near Covent Garden underground station.*

b Answer these questions about the text.

1 What was on the east side of the piazza before the 1970s?
2 Can you take children to the museum?
3 What can they do?
4 Can you buy anything at the museum? What can you buy, do you think?

Speaking

5 a 📼 Listen. Where in Covent Garden are the people?

b 💬 Work with a partner. Make a short dialogue about another place in Covent Garden. Act it out for another pair. Can they say where you are?

6 💬 Work in groups. Think of a small part of a town in your country which has got some interesting places in it. Discuss the questions.

What is the name of the area? What interesting places can you find there? Why are they interesting? What can you do in them? When are they open?

Writing

7 Prepare a tourist guide.

a In your groups, decide on which places from Exercise 6 you want to put in your tourist guide.

b Draw a simple map of the part of the town. Write a number for each place.

8 Look at the Covent Garden map and texts again.

a What sort of information is there in the map labels? Tick the first boxes.

		map labels	text
1	where the place is	☐	☐
2	the history of the place	☐	☐
3	what you can find there	☐	☐
4	what you can do there	☐	☐
5	its opening hours	☐	☐
6	its telephone number	☐	☐

b What sort of information is there in the text? Tick the second boxes.

9 a In your groups, write the labels for your map.

b Write one text each. Use the text about the London Transport Museum to help you. Write each text on a separate piece of paper.

10 Make a small guide with your map and texts.

Activities for pages 21, 35, 66, 83 and 107

Page 21 Exercise 7

Read your partner's description. Find the name of the animal.

1 stick insect

2 tree frog

3 Arctic fox

4 glass lizard

5 giraffe

6 spider

Page 35 Exercise 5

A You work in a shop. Look at the list of things in the shop. What have you got? Answer B's questions:

Yes, I have.
Or
No, sorry, I haven't got any …
Tell B about other things in the shop:
But would you like any …? I've got some good/large …

Rice
Chicken legs
Brown bread
6 large tomatoes
Cheese
Sugar
Salt
A large lettuce
12 bananas
10 onions

Page 66 Exercise 2

Are you a couch potato?

Add up your scores.

1	**a** 1	**b** 3	**c** 5	
2	**a** 1	**b** 3		
3	**a** 3	**b** 1		
4	**a** 3	**b** 5	**c** 2	**d** 1
5	**a** 5	**b** 3	**c** 1	
8	**a** 1	**b** 3	**c** 5	

What do your scores mean?

0–13 You're a real couch potato! Do you take any exercise? Do you eat any healthy food? What can you do about your lifestyle?

14–22 You're average. You eat healthy food a lot of the time and you take some exercise, but sometimes you eat unhealthy food. Don't worry!

23–26 Are you real? You only eat healthy food and you exercise all the time. Do you ever have fun?

Page 83 Exercise 1

B Read Gemma's diary about that evening and listen to A's story. Is A's story right?

> **Friday 18th August**

I waited for a long time at the bus-stop for Alex. I was tired and angry. Then the bus arrived and so I went home without Alex.

When I arrived at our flat about half an hour later, I opened the door and went in. I really hoped to find Alex there, but she wasn't. The flat was dark and my parents weren't there either. I was really worried now. I went into the kitchen and there was a message for me on the table: "The police called – something about Alex at the airport! Why? We are very worried. Please stay here and wait". After that I waited and worried about Alex for nearly two hours. I didn't want to read or watch TV – I just watched the clock. I was really tired.

Page 107 Exercise 4

B You are Kevin's friend. Write four more plans in your diary.

	Morning	Afternoon	Evening
Monday	School	School	
Tuesday	School	School	Playing volleyball
Wednesday	School	School	
Thursday	School	School	
Friday	School	School	Visiting my grandmother
Saturday			
Sunday